BUSINESS INTELLIGENCE – SOLUTION FOR BUSINESS DEVELOPMENT

Edited by **Marinela Mircea**

Business Intelligence – Solution for Business Development
Edited by Marinela Mircea

Published by InTech
Janeza Trdine 9, 51000 Rijeka, Croatia

Publishing Process Manager Daria nahtigal

Technical Editor Teodora Smiljanic

Cover Designer InTech Design Team

Additional hard copies can be obtained from orders@intechopen.com

Business Intelligence – Solution for Business Development, Edited by Marinela Mircea
p. cm.
ISBN 978-953-51-0019-5

For EU product safety concerns:
IN TECH d.o.o., Prolaz Marije Krucifikse Kozulić 3, 51000 Rijeka, Croatia,
info@intechopen.com or visit our website at intechopen.com.

Meet the editor

Marinela Mircea received her degree in Informatics in Economy from the Academy of Economic Studies, Bucharest in 2003. In February 2009, she finished the doctoral stage. Her PhD thesis is entitled "Business management in digital economy". She is teaching at Academy of Economic Studies in Bucharest, at Economic Informatics Department since 2003. Her work focuses on programming, information system, business management and Business Intelligence. Dr. Mircea has published over 60 papers and journal articles in computer science, informatics and business management field. She also served as conference organizing chair, member of program committees and reviewed several papers for international conferences. She is the author of one book and coauthor of six books. Dr. Mircea was a member of over 15 research projects, and project manager for the national research project titled "Modern Approaches in Business Intelligence Systems Development for Services-Oriented Organizations Management".

Contents

Preface

The last decades have seen multiple collisions between traditional activities on one side and technologies that undergo permanent transformations and improvements on the other side. The continuous expansion of the Business Intelligence solutions (BI) is of particular interest. Scholars and practitioners focused on the benefits of using BI solutions for business management, creating new applications, technologies and finding opportunities for performance improvement. In this context, a natural consequence is the increased interest for the possibility of adapting the organization to the electronic environment and automating the decision making process. In the new economy, this becomes a requirement too. Considering the business trend towards digitization, more and more management activities performed by informational systems of the organization, using high performance software solutions becomes a need rather than an option.

The work comes as a helpful tool in solving the complex problems facing the management activity and BI system developers in the digital economy environment. The book is the result of theoretical research and also practical experience of international experts in the field of information and communication technology and management. It provides theoretical foundation, models, solutions and case studies that build up the framework for filling the gap between theory and practice and increasing the maturity of BI solutions.

The book addresses to a large pool of readers and specialists in software development, as well as beneficiaries of BI systems, who are making it an important scientific contribution. It has an accessible style, making it useful for students and PhD candidates, professors, software developers, economists as well as managers that want to adapt their organizations to the new business environment.

The book is written in a gradual, concise and coherent manner, covering both managerial aspects (the maturity of the BI solution in the organization, integration of the BI solution with other modern solutions/technologies in order to achieve organization agility), and technological aspects (methodological approaches and proposed development solutions). The book covers a large area, including: ◎ constructing an enterprise business intelligence maturity model; ◎ developing an agile architecture framework that leverages the strengths of BI, decision management and service orientation; ◎ adding semantics to Business Intelligence; ◎ towards Business Intelligence over unified structured and unstructured data using XML; ◎ density-based clustering and anomaly detection; ◎ data mining based on neural networks.

The work helps the organizations by providing a maturity model for the BI solution and integration solutions with other technologies, aiming to achieve the organization agility and further economic innovation. The results presented here allow organizations to know the current state of BI implementation and the strategy to achieve a higher level of BI performance. The BI maturity model presented in this book serves as a guide for planning and understanding BI initiatives on a large scale. The two types of representations used in creating the model (staged representation and continuous representation) ensure measuring both the maturity and the capabilities of the key process areas. Making use of the BI experts' opinions on exploring and identifying key process areas adds to the validity of the proposed model.

The complexity of the business environment raises a series of problems for the decision making process, which lead to the need to use BI solutions combined with other solutions like decision management, service-oriented architecture and cloud computing. The present book analyzes the combined utility of these solutions, which extends the capabilities of existing systems and creates the premises for intelligent organizations. Organizations will be able to connect every level in real time in order to process daily tasks and make strategic decisions. Even more, using cloud computing solutions in the context of the economic crisis, will allow the adoption of analytical and BI solutions with low usage costs.

The increasing volume of data in the organization and its heterogeneity raise challenges for the flexibility of analytical instruments, data interpretation and personalized presenting of results. Using Semantic Business Intelligence (SBI) architecture allows the integration of business semantic, heterogeneous data sources and knowledge engineering tools that support making intelligent decisions. This has proved it usefulness in several e-gov projects for publishing data and as support for decision making. The SBI solution presented in this book provides additional capabilities for BI solutions and allows the alignment of business logic with decision making requirements.

The organization may have a large amount of unstructured data that cannot be represented in a relational model. The solution is to use an XML enabled RDBMS that uses XML as the underlying logical data model to uniformly represent both well-structured relational data and unstructured data. The book argues that such an approach has the potential to push business intelligence over all enterprise data to a new era. The management of XML in an extended Relational Database Management system is benefited by the leverage of secular DBMS technologies, such as data partition, parallel query execution and server clustering operating environments.

Data mining is used more and more alongside BI solutions and decision support systems. Use of these instruments provides capabilities for data exploration and modeling. It is difficult for the human user to detect and follow the important characteristics in very large data sets. Clustering is a data mining technique in which finite samplings of points are grouped into sets of similar points. Clustering and outlier detection is a useful and challenging problem. The present book analyzes various techniques based on density and describes their applications. Also, density based methods are compared to hierarchical and partitioning methods for discovering clusters with arbitrary shape and outlier detection. According to the results obtained, the OPTICS and LDBSCAN are the most successful due to their accuracy and the ability to effectively discover clusters with different local density.

Use of neural networks in data mining has proven to be benefic. Although neural networks have a complex structure and need a long training time, they are being used more and more in analyses and prediction. The book presents case study that highlights the positive results of using data mining techniques in providing advance information for forecast of sub-grid phenomenon.

Throughout the book, the theoretical presentation is enriched with examples, case studies and proposed solutions for increasing the performance of BI systems. The chapters integrate in a single coherent work that helps know and understand the trends in the BI field and also help form future specialists.

Lecturer Marinela Mircea, Ph.D.
Department of Economic Informatics and Cybernetics
The Bucharest Academy of Economic Studies,
Romania

1

Construct an Enterprise Business Intelligence Maturity Model (EBI2M) Using an Integration Approach: A Conceptual Framework

Min-Hooi Chuah and Kee-Luen Wong
University Tunku Abdul Rahman, Malaysia

1. Introduction

Today, Business Intelligence (BI) play an essential role particular in business areas. The important role can be seen as the BI applications have appeared the top spending priority for many Chief Information Officers (CIO) and it remain the most important technologies to be purchased for past five years(Gartner Research 2007; 2008; 2009). In fact, various market researchers including Gartner Research and International Data Corporation (IDC), forecast that the BI market will be in strong growth till 2014 (Richardson et.al , 2008).

Although there has been a growing interest in BI area, success for implementing BI is still a questionable (Ang & Teo 2000; Lupu et.al (1997); Computerworld (2003)). Lupu et.al (1997) reported that about 60%-70% of business intelligence applications fail due to the technology, organizational, cultural and infrastructure issues. Furthermore, EMC Corporation argued that many BI initiatives have failed because tools weren't accessible through to end users and the result of not meeting the end users' need effectively. Computerworld (2003) stated that BI projects fail because of failure to recognize BI projects as cross organizational business initiatives, unengaged business sponsors, unavailable or unwilling business representatives, lack of skilled and available staff, no business analysis activities, no appreciation of the impact of dirty data on business profitability and no understanding of the necessity for and the use of meta-data. A maturity model is needed to provide systematic maturity guidelines and readiness assessment for such resourceful initiative. While there are many BI maturity models in the literature but most of them do not consider all factors affecting on BI. Some of BI maturity models focus on the technical aspect and some of the models focus on business point of view.

Therefore, this research seeks to bridge this missing gap between academia and industry, through a thorough formal study of the key dimensions and associated factors pertaining to Enterprise Business Intelligence (EBI). It aims to investigate the dimensions and associated factor for each maturity level. The remainder of this paper has been structured as follows. The next section discusses the components of Business Intelligence (BI), Capability Maturity Model (CMMI) as well as review of BI maturity models. The third section then outlines and discusses the proposed EBIM model, then follows by empirical research.

2. Literature review

2.1 Definition of business intelligence

The concept of BI is very new and there is no commonly agreed definition of BI. In view of this, this section presents the various definitions and categories of BI.

Table 1 summarised various other definitions of BI have come from leading vendors and prominent authors.

BI vendor/Author	Definition of BI
Reinschmidt and Francoise (2000)	An integrated set of tools, technologies and programmed products that are used to collect, integrate, analyze and make data available
Golfarelli et.al (2004)	Process of turning data into information and knowledge.
Raisinghani (2004)	An umbrella term that includes architecture, tools, database, application and methodologies.
Chang (2006)	The accurate, timely, critical data, information and knowledge that supports strategic and operational decision making and risk assessment in uncertain and dynamic business environments. The source of the data, information and knowledge are both internal organisationally collected as well as externally supplied by partners, customers or third parties as a result of their own choice.
Zeng et.at (2006)	A set of powerful tool and approaches to improve business executive decision making, business operations and increasing the value of the enterprise.
Xu et.al (2007)	Process of gathering enough of the right information in the right manner at the right time, and delivering the right results to the right people for decision making
Jourdan (2008)	Process that analyses the information which resides in the company in order to improve its decision making process and consequently create a competitive advantage for the company.

Table 1. Summary of varied BI definitions

The term Business Intelligence (BI) can be divided into two terms: "business" and "intelligence". According to Turban et.al (2011), BI can defined as "*discipline that combines services, applications, and technologies to gather, manage, and analyze data, transforming it into usable information to develop the insight and understanding needed to make informed decisions*" while Vercellis (2009) stated that BI is a "*set of mathematical models and analysis methodologies that exploits the available data to generate information and knowledge useful for complex decision making processes*". BI can

BI can be viewed as three perspectives: technological standpoint, managerial standpoint and product standpoint. From the managerial standpoint, Whitehorn & Whitehorn (1999) illustrated BI as "*a process that focuses on gathering data from internal and external sources and analysing them in order to generate relevant information*". From product standpoint, Chang (2006) described BI can viewed as "*result or product of detailed business data as well as analysis practices that support decision-making and performance assessment*". From the technological standpoint, BI can be named as BI systems and is considered as a *"tool that enables decision makers to find or access information from data sources"* (Hostmann 2007; Moss & Atre 2003; Moss & Hoberman 2004).

2.2 The business intelligence's architecture

Turban et. al (2011) classified BI system as four main components: a data warehousing environment, business analytics, business performance management (BPM) and a user interface such as the dashboard.

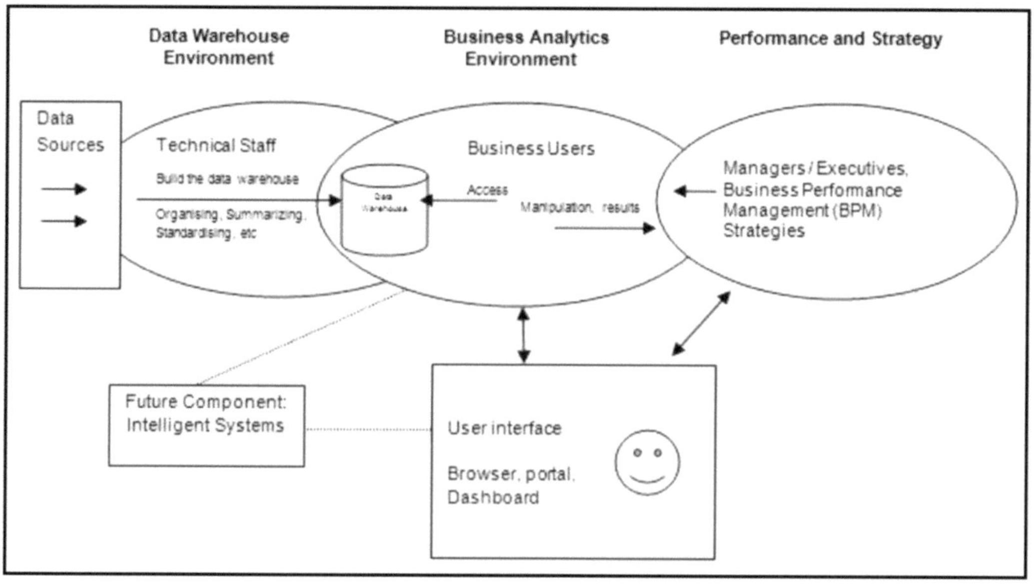

Source: Turban et.al (2011)

Fig. 1. Business Intelligence system architecture

2.2.1 Data warehousing

Data Warehousing is main component of business intelligence. Data warehousing has four fundamental characteristics namely subject oriented, integrated, time variant, non-volatile (Inmon, 2005).

i. Subject oriented
   Data are structured by specified subject such as sales, products or customers, including only information pertinent for decision support.
ii. Integrated
   All data from different department, such as sales department's data, financial data or customer's data must combine and integrated.
iii. Time Variant
   Data Warehouse stores historical data.
iv. Non Volatile
   After data loaded to data warehouse, users cannot change or update the data.

Extract, Transform and Load (ETL) is main process in data warehouse. Basically, ETL consists of three three steps: extract, transform and load. Extracting is the process of gathering the data from different data source, changed into useful information so that they can use for decision making (Reinschmidt and Francoise, 2000). The data that extracted from different sources are placed to temporary areas called staging area. This can prevent data from being extracted once again if the problem occurs in the loading process (Ranjan, 2009). Next, transformation process take place where data is cleaned, remove errors exist on data such as inconsistencies between data, redundant data, inaccurate data, and missing value and convert to into a consistent format for reporting and analysis (Ranjan, 2009). Loading is the final step of ETL where data is loaded into target repository (Ranjan, 2009).

2.2.2 Business analytics

Business analytics environment is the second core component in BI where online analytical processing (OLAP) tools are located to enable users to generate on-demand reports and queries in addition to conduct analysis of data (Turban et.al, 2011).

Codd et.al (1993) proposed that there are 12 rules for OLAP:

i. Multidimensional conceptual view for formulating queries
   OLAP must view in multidimensional. For example, profits could be viewed by region, product, time or budget
ii. Transparency to the user
   OLAP should be part of an open system architecture that allows user embedded to any part of the system without affect the functionality of the host tool.
iii. Easy accessibility
   OLAP capable of applying its own logical structure that allows users easy to access various sources of data
iv. Consistent reporting performance
   OLAP able to provide consistent reports to users
v. Client/server architecture: the use of distributed resources
   OLAP consists of client and server architectures. The servers are able to map and consolidate data from different departments.
vi. Generic dimensionality
   OLAP consists of multidimensional and every data dimension should be equivalent in its structure and operational capabilities.
vii. Dynamic sparse matrix handling
   The OLAP server's physical structure should have optimal sparse matrix handling.
viii. Multi-user support rather than support for only a single user
   OLAP tools must provide concurrent retrieval and update access, integrity and security.
ix. Unrestricted cross-dimensional operations
   OLAP consists of computational facilities that allow calculation and data manipulation across any number of data dimensional.
x. Intuitive data manipulation
   OLAP allows data manipulation in the consolidation path, such as drilling down or zooming out
xi. Flexible reporting
   OLAP consists of reporting facilities that can present information in any way the user wants to view it.

Turban et.al (2011) stated there are five basic OLAP operations that can be used to analyse multidimensional data, such as:

- Roll-up or drill-up
  - It allows user to view more summarised information for a given data cube. This can be carried out by moving down to lower levels of details and grouping one of the dimensions together to summarize data.
- Drill-down
  - It is the opposite of roll-up, which is used to view more detailed information by moving upwards to higher levels of details for a given data cube.
- Slice
  - It allows the users to select and analyse specific value of a cube's dimension.
- Dice
  - To analyse data, users can select many dimensions at the same time to view single value in data cube.
- Pivot
  - It enables user to rotate the axes of the data cube, meaning that change the dimensions to get different views of data.

Besides using OLAP, data mining or predictive analysis can be used to analyze data and information in more practical way. Data mining, also called knowledge discovery, is technique to discovery the unknown or unusual patterns from huge database. Predictive analysis is method that used to forecast the future outcome for an occasion or possibility of circumstances will happen

2.2.3 Business Performance Management

Business performance management (BPM) is component or methodology that used by an organisation to measure the performance of an organization in general. BPM usually can be visualised by portal, dashboard or scorecard.

2.2.4 User interface

Portal, web browser, dashboard and scorecard are used to view organization's performance measurement from numerous business areas. Dashboard and scorecard uses visual components such as charts, performance bars, and gauges to highlight data to the user. They provide drill down or drill up capability to enable the user to view the data more clearly and conveniently.

2.3 Capability Maturity Model (CMM)

The concept of Capability Maturity Model (CMM) was initially raised by Watts Humphrey at Software Engineering Institute (SEI), Carnegie Mellon University in 1986. CMM is used in software development and it can provide the guideline, step by step for process improvement across a project, a division, or an entire enterprise (Paulk et al., 2006). CMM offers a set of guidelines to improve an organisation's processes within an important area (Wang & Lee 2008).

Basically, CMM consists of five maturity level, which are level 1 : initial; level2: repeatable; level 3: defined, level 4 : ,managed and level 5 : optimizing.

In the initial level, processes are uncontrolled, disorganised, ad-hoc. Project outcomes are depend on individual efforts. In Repeatable level, project management processes are defined. Planning and managing new projects based on the experience with similar project. In Defined level, the organisation has developed own processes, which are documented and used while in Managed level, quality management procedures are defined. The organisation monitors and controls its own process through data collection and analysis. In optimizing level, processes are constantly being improved (Paulk et.al, 2006).

CMMs have been developed in many disciplines area such as systems engineering, software engineering, software acquisition, workforce management and development, and integrated product and process development (IPPD). The utilization of various models that are not integrated within an organization in terms of their architecture, content, and approach, have created redundancy as an organisation need separate model to measure different disciplines areas.

Thus, Capability Maturity Model Integration (CMMI) was derived in 2000 and it is an improved version of the CMM. CMMI is an integrated model that combines three source models which consist of *Capability Maturity Model for Software* (SW-CMM) v2.0, the *Systems Engineering Capability Model* (SECM), the *Integrated Product Development Capability Maturity Model* (IPD-CMM).

2.4 Business Intelligence Maturity Model

There are numerous Business Intelligence maturity model developed by different authors such as Business intelligence Development Model (BIDM), TDWI's maturity model, Business Intelligence Maturity Hierarchy, Hewlett Package Business Intelligence Maturity Model, Gartner's Maturity Model, Business Information Maturity Model, AMR Research's Business Intelligence/ Performance Management Maturity Model, Infrastructure Optimization Maturity Model and Ladder of business intelligence (LOBI). This section reviewed several of business intelligence maturity models by different authors.

Maturity models	Description
TDWI's maturity model	• The maturity assessment tool is available in the web to evaluate BI's maturity level as well as documentation. • Concentrates on the technical viewpoints especially in data warehouse aspect. • Can be improved on business viewpoint especially from the cultural and organizational view.
Business Intelligence Maturity Hierarchy	• Applied the knowledge management field • Author constructed maturity levels from a technical point of view but can considered as incomplete. • The documentation of this model in the form of one paper and is not enough for maturity level assessment.

Maturity models	Description
Hewlett Package Business Intelligence Maturity Model	• Depicts the maturity levels from business technical aspect. • This model is new and need to improve to add more technical aspects such as data-warehousing and analytical aspects.
Gartner's Maturity Model	• Uses to evaluate the business maturity levels and maturity of individual departments. • Provides more non technical view and concentrates on the business technical aspect. • Well documented and can search easily on the Web. • The assessment offers the series of questionnaire to form of spreadsheet.
Business Information Maturity Model	• Well documented with the series of questionnaire to assist the users to perform self evaluation. • However, criteria to evaluate the maturity level are not well defined.
AMR Research's Business Intelligence/ Performance Management Maturity Model	• Concentrates on the performance management and balanced scorecard rather than business intelligence. • Not well documented and criteria to evaluate the maturity level are not well defined. • No questionnaire to evaluate the maturity levels and is very hard to analysis the model (Rajteric, 2010).
Infrastructure Optimization Maturity Model	• Focuses on the measurement of the efficiency of reporting, analysis and data-warehousing and is not complete in the business intelligence area (Rajteric, 2010). • Discuss about the products and technologies rather than business point of view (Rajteric, 2010). • Not well documented and criteria to evaluate the maturity level are not well defined.
Ladder of business intelligence (LOBI)	• Apply the knowledge management field • Author constructed maturity levels from a technical point of view but can considered as incomplete. • Not well documented and criteria to evaluate the maturity level are not well defined.
Business intelligence Development Model (BIDM)	• Not well documented and criteria to evaluate the maturity level are not well defined. • Concentrates on the technical aspects rather than business point of view

Table 2. Summary of various maturity models

Table 2 above depicts summary of various business intelligence maturity models. As shown in the table 2 above, the majority of the models do not focus the business intelligence as entire which some of models focus on the technical aspect and some of the models focus on business point of view. For example, TDWI's model only concentrates on the data warehousing while Business Intelligence Maturity Hierarchy only concentrates on knowledge management. It is not complete to represent business intelligence. We know that business intelligence covers not only data warehousing, but also business performance, balanced scorecard, analytical components.

In addition, the documentation of some maturity models above is not well defined and they do not provide any guidelines or questionnaire to evaluate maturity levels. From example, only TDWI's maturity model provides questionnaire and assessment tool on the web while other BI maturity model such as Business Intelligence Maturity Hierarchy, Hewlett Package Business Intelligence Maturity Model, Gartner's Maturity Model, Business Information Maturity Model, AMR Research's Business Intelligence/ Performance Management Maturity Model, Infrastructure Optimization Maturity Model, Ladder of business intelligence (LOBI) and Business Intelligence Development Model (BIDM) do not provide any guidelines or questionnaire to evaluate maturity levels.

Since the majority of the models do not focus the business intelligence as entire which some of models focus on the technical aspect and some of the models focus on business point of view, if the organizations want to know exact their business intelligence maturity levels as whole, they have to use multiple models and that it is time consuming. Therefore, there is need to have an integrated maturity model to consolidate existing different maturity models. In view of this, an Enterprise Business Intelligence Maturity model (EBI2M) is proposed.

3. Proposed Enterprise Business Intelligence Maturity model (EBIM)

Based on the literature review in the section 2.3, a preliminary version of an enterprise business intelligence maturity model (EBI2M) is developed. The proposed EBI2M's structure is borrowed from the CMMI concept. There are two main reasons to justify the use of CMMI model in the EBI implementation. First, the CMMI maturity structure is generic enough to provide a more holistic integration approach (Paulk et.al, 2006) as compared to CMM. Secondly, CMMI consists of two representations: staged representation and continuous representation while other maturity model such as CMM consists of only staged representation. Continuous representation is necessary for providing organizations with the freedom to select the order of improvement that best meets the organization's requirement (Paulk et.al, 2006).

The proposed EBI2M consists of two representations: staged representation and continuous representation. The staged representation consists of five levels namely; initial, managed, defined, quantitatively managed and optimizing; all of which are adapted from CMMI maturity levels.

Figure 2 depicts the stage representation of the proposed EBI2M.

In the level 1 (initial), there is no process area and process is chaotic.

Level 2 (managed) concentrates on the change management, organization culture, and people.

Level 3(defined level) is the level where EBI implementation processes are documented, standardized, and integrated into a standard implementation process for the organization.

This level contains data warehousing, master data management, analytical, infrastructure and knowledge management

In level 4 (quantitatively managed level) EBI process and activities are controlled and managed based on quantitative models and tools. Hence performance management, balanced scorecard, information quality factors are placed at this level.

Level 5 (optimizing level) is the level where organizations establish structures for continuous improvement and contains strategic management factor.

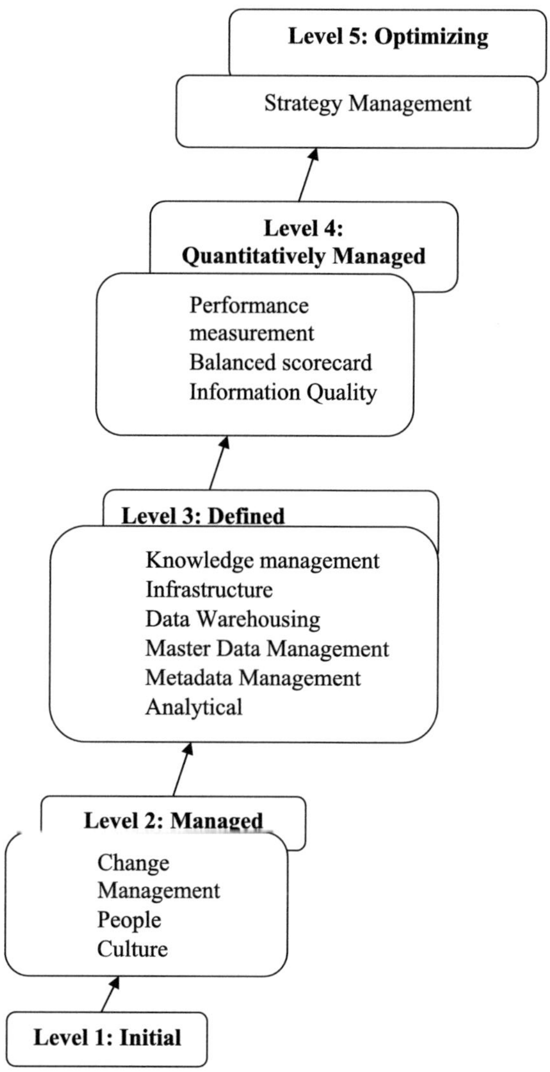

Developed by author

Fig. 2. Proposed staged representation of Enterprise Business Intelligence Maturity model (EBI2M)

A staged representation of EBI2M can be reasonably mapped in five evolutionary levels as shown in figure 2. Each maturity level is a prerequisite to the next higher one. Therefore each higher maturity level encompasses all previous lower levels. For instance, a company at level 3 maturity level embraces the important factors of level 1 and 2.

The continuous representation consists of thirteen dimensions: change management, organization culture, strategic management, people, performance management, balanced scorecard, information quality, data warehousing, master data management, metadata management, analytical, infrastructure and knowledge management.

As discussed in the literature review, data warehousing, master data management, metadata management, analytical, infrastructures, performance management, balanced scorecard are the main components in business intelligence architecture. Therefore, these seven factors (data warehousing, master data management, metadata management, analytical, infrastructures, performance management, and balanced scorecard) should be considered for key maturity indicators for EBI2M.

In order to be success in the implementing of BI, organization need to ensure they can adapt to the any changes in the organization, people or knowledge workers have good skills and they willing to face any challenges. Besides that, organization must analyze their strengths and weakness and competitors' strengths and weakness.

Change management, organization culture, strategic management and people are chosen for key maturity indicators for EBI2M with rationale organization need to ensure they can adapt to the any changes in the organization, people or knowledge workers have good skills and willing to face any challenges. Besides that, in order to be success in the implementing of BI, organization must analyze their strengths and weakness and competitors' strengths and weakness.

Information quality or data quality is another factor to be considered for key maturity indicators for EBI2M. Organization must make sure that the data that entered to data warehouse is clean and no redundancy occurs.

The advantage of having continuous representation in EBI2M is that it allows organization to measure the dimensions independently. For example, if organization wants to measure capabilities of change management of independently, they can use continuous representation in EBI2M.

4. Methodology

The Stage 1 Delphi study is used to narrow down the scope of this research because of limited academic literature. The rationale of choosing Delphi study in this research is due to lack of complete information and limitation of literature review especially on business intelligence maturity model. Therefore, there is need for experts to explore and identify the key process areas so that these opinions can be useful to construct maturity models. Furthermore, by using Delphi method, experts do not involve in a face by face discussion; so, there is little chance of one of more individuals' opinions being influenced by more experience individual. Moreover, compare to other method such as focus group, Delphi was used due to geographical location. It is not convenient for all expert panels to gather together due to the time constraint and location constraint.

Around 15 BI experts were chosen through various BI forums in Linkedin Connections. These BI experts were chosen based on their experience on BI. Table II shows the experiences of 15 participants.

Participants	Positions	Years of experiences in BI
1	Data Warehouse Architect	6 - 7 years
2	Manager DW/BI	10 years and above
3	IT Support Executive	6 - 7 years
4	Business Intelligence/Data Architect	10 years and above
5	Senior IS Manager	6 - 7 years
6	Vice President	10 years and above
7	CIO	4 - 5 years
8	Vice President (IT)	10 years and above
9	BI manager	10 years and above
10	BI / DW Architect	10 years and above
11	Functional Analyst	8 - 9 years
12	ETL Developer	6 - 7 years
13	Data Warehouse Lead Architect	10 years and above
14	Manager	10 years and above
15	Director	6 - 7 years

Table 3. Delphi study's participate

In the first round of Delphi study, the series of questionnaire distributed to 15 participants. The participants are asked to map the key process area (change management, culture, strategic management, people, performance measurement, balanced scorecard, information quality, data warehousing, metadata management, master data management, analytical, infrastructure and knowledge management) to suitable the maturity levels.

5. Preliminary results

Delphi study results were analyzed using descriptive statistics, including the median and the interquartile range. Interquartile ranges are usually used in Delphi studies to show the degree of group consensus. When using a 5-point Likert scale, responses with a quartile deviation less than or equal to 0.6 can be deemed high consensus, those greater than 0.6 and less than or equal to 1.0 can be deemed moderate consensus, and those greater than 1.0 should be deemed low consensus (Raskin, 1994; Faherty, 1979).

Table 4 depicts the Delphi study round1's result. As shown in table 4, only 'Infrastructure' achieve strong consensus. Change management, organization culture, performance measurement, people, balanced scorecard, information quality, metadata management, master data management and knowledge management achieve moderate consensus. The other key process area such as analytical do not achieve consensus among the Delphi panels. Therefore, 'Infrastructure' is shortlisted in subsequent round.

The median values were used to indicate the preferred Capability Maturity level for each Maturity Indicator, where 1 indicates the lowest and 5 the highest Maturity level. For example, 'Infrastructure' is short listed and placed in maturity level 3.

Key Process Area	Medium	Interquartile
Change management	3	1
Organization Culture	2	1
Strategic Management	4	2
People	3	1
Performance Measurement	4	1
Balanced Scorecard	3	1
Information Quality	3	1
Data Warehousing	3	2
Master Data Management	3	1
Metadata Management	4	1
Analytical	3	2
Infrastructure	3	0
Knowledge Management	4	1

Table 4. Delphi study round 1's result

6. Conclusion and future works

This paper proposed an enterprise business intelligence maturity model (EBI2M). The purpose of EBI2M is assisting the enterprise on BI implementation. This research is the preliminary endeavour at identifying the dimensions and associated factors influencing EBI maturity. Based on the maturity constructs of CMMI and relevant literature of BI, the concept of EBI maturity was explored and defined.

This research is benefit to the enterprises or organizations because it enables the organizations to know their current BI implementation status and how to achieve the higher level of BI implementation. Amongst the findings, this paper indicates that only key process area 'Infrastructure' achieve strong consensus by all Delphi panels. In the future, the subsequent round will be conducted to ensure that all key process areas achieve consensus among the Delphi panels.

7. Acknowledgment

The authors acknowledge the time and commitment of all members of the Delphi Study for their useful contributions.

8. References

Ang, J & Teo, TSH 2000, 'Management Issues in Data Warehousing: Insights from the Housing and Development Board', Decision Support Systems, vol. 29, no. 1, pp. 11-20.

Cates, J.E., Gill, S.S., Zeituny, N. 2005, The Ladder of Business Intelligence (LOBI): a framework for enterprise IT planning and architecture, *International Journal of Business Information system*, vol. 1, no : 1, pp220-238.

Chang, E 2006, 'Advanced BI Technologies, Trust, Reputation and Recommendation Systems', presented at the 7th Business Intelligence Conference (Organised by Marcus Evans), Sydney, Australia.

Codd, E.F., Codd S.B and Salley, C.T 1993, 'Beyond Decision Support', Computerworld.

Computerworld, 2003, 'The top 10 Critical Challenges for Business Intelligence Success', Computerworld.

Deng, R., 2007. Business Intelligence Maturity Hierarchy: A New Perspective from Knowledge Management. Information Management. http://www.information-management.com/ infodirect/20070323/1079089-1.html

Eckerson, W. 2004, 'Gauge Your Data Warehouse Maturity', *Information management,* viewed on 29. April 2009, <http://www.information-management.com/issues/20041101/1012391-1.html>.

Faherty, V. 1979, Continuing social work education: Results of a Delphi surved, *Journal of Education for Social Work*, 1979. 15(1): p. 12-19.

Gartner Research 2007, "Gartner EXP Survey of More than 1,400 CIOs Shows CIOs Must Create Leverage to Remain Relevant to the Business." Retrieved 01/04/2009, from <http://www.gartner.com/it/page.jsp?id=501189>.

Gartner Research 2008, "Gartner EXP Worldwide Survey of 1,500 CIOs Shows 85 Percent of CIOs Expect "Significant Change" Over Next Three Years." Retrieved 01/04/2009, from <http://www.gartner.com/it/page.jsp?id=587309>.

Gartner Research 2009, "Gartner EXP Worldwide Survey of More than 1,500 CIOs Shows IT Spending to Be Flat in 2009." Retrieved 01/04/2009, from <http://www.gartner.com/it/page.jsp?id=855612>.

Golfarelli, M., Rizzi, S and Cella, I. 2004, Beyond data warehousing: what's next in business intelligence? *Proceedings of the 7th ACM international workshop on Data warehousing and OLAP*, pp.1-pp.6.

Hagerty, J. 2006, *AMR Research's Business Intelligence/ Performance Management Maturity Model, Version 2,* viewed on 21 April 2009, <http://www.cognos.com/pdfs/analystreports/ar_amr_researchs_bi_perf.pdf >.

Hostmann, B 2007, 'Business Intelligence Scenario ', paper presented at the Gartner Business Intelligence Summit, London.

IDC 2007, Top Ranked Business Intelligence Tools Vendors Maintain Positions, viewed 03 Jul 2007, <http://www.idc.com/getdoc.jsp?containerId=prUS20767807>.

Jourdan, Z., Rainer, R.K., and Marshall, T.E. 2008. Business intelligence: An analysis of the literature. *Information Systems Management*, 25, 2, 121-131.

Kašnik, A. 2008, 'Model optimization infrastructure', *Internal material of ZRSZ,* Ljubljana.

Lupu, A.M., Bologa, R., Lungu, I and Bra, A 2007, 'The impact of organization changes on business intelligence projects', Proceedings of the 7th WSEAS International Conference on Simulation, Modeling and Optimization, Beijing, China, September 15-17, pp.414-418.

Moss, L & Atre, S 2003, Business Intelligence Roadmap: The Complete Lifecycle for Decision-Support Applications. , Addison-Wesley, Boston, MA.

Moss, L & Hoberman, S 2004, *The Importance of Data Modeling as a Foundation for Business Insight*, Teradata.

Paulk, MC, Curtis, B, Chrissis, MB & Weber, CV 2006, *Capability Maturity Model for Software, Version 1.2,* Software Engineering Institute/Carnegie Mellon University.

Raisinghani, M. 2004. *Business Intelligence in the Digital Economy: Opportunities, Limitations and Risks*, Hershey, PA: The Idea Group.

Rajterič, I.H., 2010. Overview of Business Intelligence Maturity Models. International *Journal of Human Science*, vol 15, no :1, pp 47-67.

Ranjan, V 2009, A comparative study between ETL (Extract, Transform, Load) and ELT(Extract, Load and Transform) approach for loading data into data warehouse, viewed 2010-03-05, http://www.ecst.csuchico.edu/~juliano/csci693/Presentations/2009w/Materials/Ranjan/Ranjan.pdf.

Raskin, M.S. 1994, The Delphi study in field instruction revisited: Expert consensus on issues and research priorities, *Journal of Social Work Education*, 1994. 30: p. 75-89.

Reinschmidt, J & Francoise, A 2000, *Business Intelligence Certification Guide*, IBM, International Technical Support Organization, San Jose, CA

Richardson, J.K., Schlegel, 2008. *Magic Quadrant for Business Intelligence Platforms*, Gartner.

Sacu, C. and Spruit, M. 2010, BIDM: The Business Intelligence Development Model. *Proceedings of the 12th International Conference on Enterprise Information Systems*, Funchal, Madeira-Portugal.

Turban, E., Sharda, R., Aronson, J. E., & D. King 2011. *Business Intelligence: A Managerial Approach*, Prentice Hall.

Vercellis, C 2009, *Business Intelligence : Data Mining and Optimization for Decision Making*. Wiley.

Wang, M H and Lee, C S 2008, 'An Intelligent PPQA Web Services for CMMI Assessment'. *Eight International Conference on Intelligent Systems Design and Applications*, (pp. 229-234).

Whitehorn, M & Whitehorn, M 1999, *Business Intelligence: The IBM Solution Datawarehousing and OLAP*, Springer-Verlag, NY.

William, S and William, N. 2007, *The Profit Impact of Business Intelligence*, Morgan Kaufmann Publishers, San Francisco.

Xu, L., Zeng, L., Shi, Z., He, Q., & Wang, M. 2007. *Research on Business Intelligence in enterprise computing environment*. Paper presented at the IEEE International Conference on Systems, Man and Cybernetics, 2007. ISIC., Montreal, QC, Canada.

Zeng, L., Xu, L., Shi, Z., Wang, M. and Wu, W. 2006, 'Techniques, process, and enterprise solutions of business intelligence', *2006 IEEE Conference on Systems, Man, and Cybernetics October 8-11, 2006, Taipei, Taiwan*, Vol. 6, pp. 4722.

2

An Agile Architecture Framework that Leverages the Strengths of Business Intelligence, Decision Management and Service Orientation

Marinela Mircea, Bogdan Ghilic-Micu and Marian Stoica
The Bucharest Academy of Economic Studies, Romania

1. Introduction

In nowadays economy, the tendency of any enterprise is to become an intelligent one and through new and innovative strategies of business intelligence (BI) obtain a competitive advantage on the market. At the same time, the collaborative environment involves the need for modern solutions to cope with the complex interactions between participants and the frequently changing market. In these circumstances, enterprises tend to go beyond agility and achieve a dynamic vision on demand. In a narrow sense, the agility incorporates ideas of flexibility, balance, adaptability and coordination. The enterprise agility may be considered the ability of the enterprise to adapt rapidly and to cost efficiently in response to changes in its operating environments (Wang & Lee, 2011; Dove, 2001). The *intelligent enterprise* is the learning enterprise where the capability to continuously adapt to changes and unpredictable environments is developed (Brătianu et al., 2006). In addition to the previous definition, we shall consider the intelligent enterprise as having a *lean, agile and learning enterprise knowledge infrastructure* as driver for sustainable competitive advantage. According to the Gartner Group, the agile enterprise must be "Real-time, service-oriented and event-controlled" (Vickoff, 2007).

Thus, within enterprises the need for proactive, challenging instruments appeared having a strong impact when compared with conventional reports, dashboards, analyses carried out by OLAP (On Line Analytical Processing) systems and this aspect may be noticed at the business intelligence suppliers. Due to the industry changes, the year 2007 marked the beginning of a new business intelligence era, proactive, extensible and performance-oriented. This new era may be viewed as a new perspective where business intelligence is combined with the management of business processes, business rules engine, decision management systems, service-oriented architecture and other instruments and techniques directly/indirectly and immediately applied to the decisions of the business. The new BI era is characterized by the following aspects:

- integrates the information within the decisional processes through decision services;
- ties business processes with business rules which may be changed any time;

- integrates the business intelligence benefits with the capabilities offered by the team, collaboration and management of business processes.

In the last stage of evolution, business intelligence can be seen as a service fully integrated with processes, applications, marketing strategies of the organization, able to solve business problems and capitalize on market opportunities. As an integrated service, business intelligence becomes from monolithic system, a flexible service, agile, able to adapt quickly to the demands and market changes. To reach the last stage of business intelligence maturity, suppliers must provide end to end platform to support the service requirements of business intelligence. Thus, suppliers should focus on the latest technologies and tools to solve problems faced and the opportunities in the market. Identification and analysis capabilities of the platform, highlighting the differences between emerging technologies capable to solve the same type of problems, highlighting trends are needs in the development of agile business intelligence platform.

A service-oriented architecture (SOA) can provide numerous benefits such as promoting reuse, the ability to combine services to create composite applications, while providing a conduit for developing technology solutions for business intelligence. Implementing master data management (MDM) ensures consistency of data in SOA strategy, aligning the organization information resources, correct dissemination of information inside/outside the organization, ensuring delivery of all the potential benefits of SOA initiatives. Complex event processing (CEP) is a technology based on rules that groups real-time information systems, databases and distributed applications to provide benefits business intelligence solution. Each organization acts as a set of rules, business rules (BR), which may be external rules (regulations in force that can be seen in all organizations operating in a particular area) and internal rules (which define the business policies of organization whose purpose).

The combination of BI, SOA, MDM, BR and CEP enables organizations to be connected in real time at each level, to process daily activities and strategic decisions. Also, in the context of a recession, the combination of cloud computing technology offers new ways and BI analytical data management and business possibilities. Cloud computing streamline BI offering hardware, networking, security and software necessary to create data on demand deposits and different approaches to pricing and licensing use. Currently, there are still issues of how to combine these technologies to provide the ability to identify and implement new solutions that take advantage of accurate real time data about products, customers and suppliers to ensure organization and coordination and proper use of information within the organization to achieve business objectives and gaining competitive advantage.

Business intelligence evolved from a data-oriented to a process-oriented model allowing for optimization of business processes based on near real-time, actionable information. Process-oriented BI combines business process management (BPM) and business intelligence (Jandi, 2008, as cited in Mircea et al., 2010) and is subordinated to upper management. It provides the input data for business decisions that execute the organization's strategy, improve performance and in the end give the best results (Ventana, 2006), applying intelligence into practice. The process-oriented BI is implemented in the entire organization, being used in business planning and in business development (tactic and operational BI) and providing information for strategic, tactic and operational decisions. At the same time, the output offered by business intelligence represent inputs for grounding the decisions related to BPM processes. The combination between BPM and BI provides many benefits, leading to simplified, efficient and agile processes, but it does not automate the decisional process, which represents an essential element to be taken into consideration in obtaining enterprise agility.

At present, the organizational expansion and the complex business environment determines the decision process to be confronted with at least the following challenges (Yu & Zheng, 2011): the complexity increase of the decisional environment, the need for some dynamically changed decisions, taking decisions based on heterogeneous and distributed decisional resources. Also, the decisional process usually takes a long time to reach a final decision (thus there is a gap between the time the information is received and the time the decision is made). Under these conditions, arises the need for a decision management (DM) solution, that extends the capabilities of existing technological solutions (for example BI, BPM, SOA) at least in these directions (FICO, 2009): ❶ gives business users control to increase agility, ❷ helps organizations make decisions in the face of uncertainty, ❸ drive out costs and ensure optimal resource allocation in the business, maximizing the return they make on their assets, ❹ helps organizations improve customer treatment everywhere.

For the success of the implementation, it is essential that the decision management to be performed using modern technologies/solutions of decision automation and optimization. It is also important that the management of these decisions to be performed alongside processes and not by using business process management. The service-oriented approach allows the automation, management and reuse of decisions as decision services in SOA. Service-oriented architecture permits the maximization of the decision's reuse, the reduction of time in taking decisions and the increase of return of investment. Moreover, service-oriented architecture facilitates the data management expansion within the entire organization. Thus, decision management becomes enterprise decision management (EDM). According to recent researches, decision management offers the biggest value when applied within the entire organization.

The objective entails development of an agile architecture framework that leverages the strengths of business intelligence, decision management and service orientation that should support solving integration problems, complex interactions between business partners and gain enterprise agility. In order to attain the agility goal we will look at three fundamental elements: data, processes and decisions. Achieving this desiderate implies knowledge on the meaning of business intelligence, business process management, decision management and service-oriented architecture, as well as understanding the connection between them.

2. Combining business intelligence with decision management

In the business context of today, characterized by high complexity and uncertainty, making the right decisions is an important process and, usually, difficult one. Even more, using collaborative solutions, based on internet and the apparition of new types of organizations (virtual organizations) changes every aspect of the business (structure, culture, processes). The new generation of business requires collaborative decisions and a new management style (Tapscott & Tapscott, 2010). The lack of adequate technological solutions to support the decisional process may lead to disastrous effects, especially for financial institutions (banks, insurance, credit, investment companies).

Over the time, business intelligence solutions were developed to help managers solve decision problems, by providing them with an analysis of a large amount of data – especially for the higher levels of the hierarchy. These solutions improve various aspects of decision making, literature dividing them into 1. strategic BI, 2. tactical BI, 3. operational BI, and 4. pervasive BI. They are designed for different categories of users, helping them make strategic, tactical and operational decisions. All four types leave the actual decision making outside the business intelligence system, where the main factors are user experience, organization rules and policy and system information.

During the recent years, organizations shifted their focus from strategic decisions (few, but with high economic impact) towards operational decisions (many, with low economic impact). In (Media, n.d.) the importance of operational decisions is highlighted as their large number compensated for the small effect, adding up or exceeding the effect of strategic decisions. Operational decisions are considered critical and the lack of ability to make them may reduce the organization's chances for success. In order to improve the operational decisions, operational or pervasive business intelligence solutions may be used. Pervasive business intelligence ensures the implementation of technologies, organizational culture and business processes aiming to improve the stakeholders' ability to make operational and strategic decisions (IDC, 2008). The decisions situated at the level of process unit (operational decisions) are the front line in driving business agility.

The automation of operational decisions can be performed by using decision management systems. They allow the identification of operational decisions, their automation, the separation and storage of decisions into a central repository. The need for automated decisions lead to the use of decision management systems that integrate policies, procedures, business rules and the best practices into making the best decisions. Decision management systems focus on the decisional process, allowing agile, precise, consistent and fast decisions with low cost.

The change in the business structure, due to collaborative environment, leads to changes in the decisional system like: more decision makers, transparency and opening (Tapscott & Tapscott, 2010). A collaborative decision management solution (CDM) fits very well to this context. Gartner Research calls this "a green field market as far as software is concerned". Table 1 (Taylor, 2009) presents various aspects of business intelligence solutions and decision management solution. Additionally, we present aspects the decision management solution in a collaborative environment (CDM).

Solution / Aspect	Strategic BI	Tactical BI	Operational BI	Pervasive BI	Decision Management	Collaborative Decision Management
Goal	Long-term planning	Manage line of business	Improve daily operations	Improve daily operations	Improve daily operations	Improve daily operations
Users	Executives, analysts	Line of business managers	Operational managers	Front-line staff	Front-line systems	Knowledge workers, and front-line systems
Response Time	Days	Hours	Minutes	Seconds	Sub-second	Faster, real time
Analysis	Long-term trends and patterns	Tracking against KPIs, investigation	Exception or problem handling	Summaries, some trending	Patterns, predictions, scoring	Technically-sophisticated analysis, sharing of experience
Decision Making	Manual	Mix of manualy and guided	Guided	None	Automated	Decentralized and optimized
Interface	Reports and documents	BI tools & applications	Dashboards	Code or BPM environment	Decision service	Decision portals
Timeliness	Weekly	Daily	Intra-day	Continuous	As needed	As needed

Table 1. A summary of different aspects of BI and decision management (Adapted from Taylor, 2009)

The importance and benefits of using a decision management solution was recognized by multiple specialists in this field. A recent study by International Data Corporation (IDC) called "Worldwide Decision management Software 2010-2014: A Fast-Growing Opportunity to Drive the Intelligent Economy" highlights three important factors of decision making process (the flow of data, faster cycle times and the adoption of analytics) and provides a systematic approach to the process of decision making across the organization (Vesset et. al., 2010). Also, the study shows that the need to increase the visibility between intra- and inter-organizational business processes will lead to the acceleration of the adoption and use of decision management solutions.

As for the use of collaborative decision management solutions, they proved their utility and benefits in various fields. A successful example is the use of collaborative decision management in air transport. British Airport Authority has chosen Pegasystems' SmartBPM platform to support Airport - Collaborative Decision Making at London Heathrow Airport (Pega, 2010). The collaborative decision making program, a concept developed by Eurocontrol – the European Air Traffic Control agency – is designed to improve the overall efficiency of operations at an airport and create a coordinated Europe-wide air traffic management system, encompassing both en route and airport operations. Also, T-Systems developed the Total Airport Management System, a modular, collaborative decision management solution which is already being used at more than 50 airports around the world (T-systems, 2010).

Currently, the rate of use of a business intelligence/analytics solution varies greatly across sectors of activity. According to a study carried out by IDC on 2271 IT managers in 2010, the adoption rate varies between 87% (the highest) in the securities and investments industry to 52% (the lowest) in education (Morris, 2010).

The combination of decision management solutions, business intelligence solutions and other technologies improves the processes, making them more responsive, more intelligent and more automated. Decision management is a subset of enterprise architecture that improves the decision making process using business rules management system (BRMS), business process management systems, business intelligence for analytics and other tools. Table 2 presents some of the main benefits brought by automation and decision improvement, as well as the technologies used.

Decision management systems create a link between historical data provided by business intelligence and foreseen results in order to make the best decision. Used together, the two solutions provide decision makers with required information about the business processes and support for automation and decision making. Enterprise data management may be considered the link from business intelligence to *intelligent business*. The adoption of enterprise decision management provides superior facilities to the business intelligence instruments through the use of new technologies like data mining and predictive analytics technologies. Also, enterprise decision management and business intelligence complete each other regarding the focus on the three decision categories. Enterprise decision management is oriented on the operational decisions, business intelligence is oriented on strategic decision and the combination of the two provides support for tactical decisions. Figure 1 depicts the complementarity and the benefits of business intelligence, business process management system (BPMS) and business rules management system (BRMS) (as support for decision automation).

Decision Management Areas	Description	Technologies
Situational awareness and decision execution	Ability to identify events that take place in the system and react to them by providing precise and robust decisions.	Business rule management system, business event processing
Analytics	Analytics features that may be used for decision improvement and execution.	Predictive analytic, neural networks, performance management, data mining
Monitoring, reporting and optimization	Ability to provide decision support to the management personnel and systems, based on historical data and current data, through a process of optimization and simulation.	Business activity monitoring, dashboards, data warehousing, optimization, simulation
Process management – operational decision	Improvement of process agility by providing the best solution from a variety of operational decision and reuse of decision logic across processes and systems.	Business process management, business rules management, decision management, business intelligence for analytics
Intelligence	Integration of intelligence in operational processes/systems, which allows prognosis and optimization in order to identify and perform the ideal action.	Business process management, decision management and BI tools
Precision, optimization, opportunity	Improvement of precision through analyses of historical data and creation of prediction and optimization models that help make the right decision.	Predictive analytic, dashboards, data warehousing, optimization, simulation

Table 2. Some benefits of decision automation and improvement

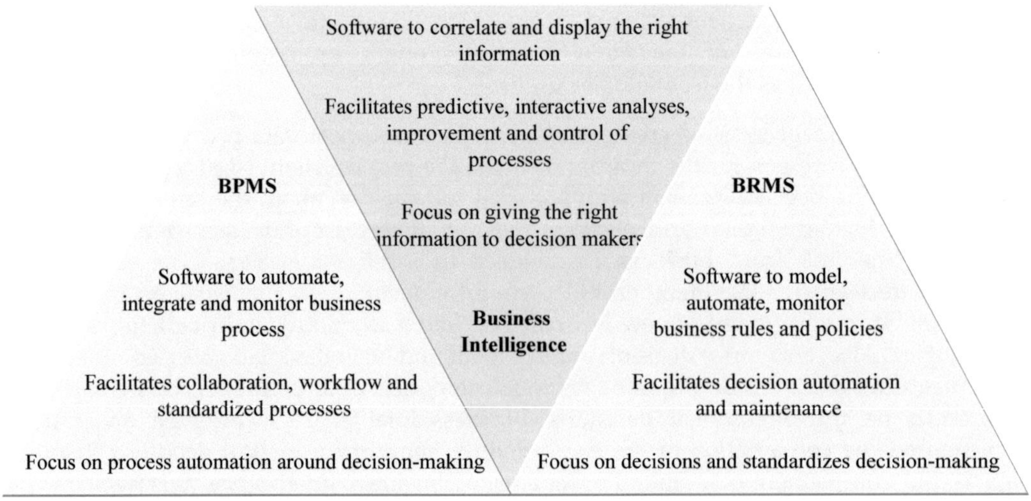

Fig. 1. Intelligent decisions from end to end

Business intelligence solutions may be used directly by the decision makers as support (guide, information provider) for decision making or indirectly by specialists as functions in the decision management. In the second case, the decision makers will interact with the decision management solution where they will define the problem and then the decision management will use the business intelligence for research and to present the results to the users. The specialists involved in various actions during the enterprise decision management chain (figure 2) can be: data analysts (for analytic models of the historical data provided by business intelligence), portfolio analysts (for optimization of strategy, based on the models created by data analysts and data about the new opportunities provided by business intelligence) and business experts that monitor and execute the business rules. Business rules management systems allow for automation of decision making based on business intelligence metrics and may take direct control of operational systems. The use of business rules management and business intelligence will ensure the support for the improvement of correctness, consistency, speed and automation of complex decisions that are facing enterprise decision management systems.

In a collaborative environment, enterprise decision management solutions must provide a few key additional features like: the decision is made by a group of decision makers from the same organization or multiple organizations; transparency of the decision making process, recording of the decision making process and self-learning; existence of collaborative decision support systems or technologies that allow the decision makers to take part in the collaborative decision making process.

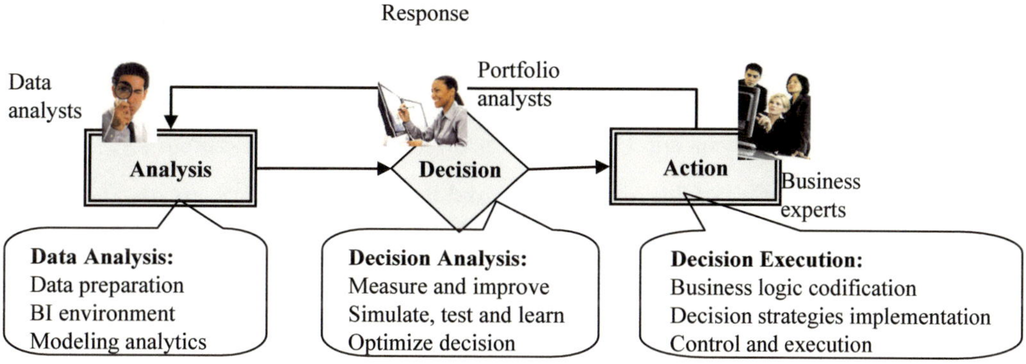

Fig. 2. The enterprise decision management chain

Combined use of business intelligence and enterprise decision management must not be seen only as potential benefits for the organization. The organization is faced with a series of problems and challenges (for example enterprise decision management interoperability with external systems) that require additional approaches / solutions. Considering this, we will look upon the analyses of service-oriented architecture, which is nowadays recognized as having benefits in solving interoperability and adaptability issues. Without service-oriented architecture, the use of enterprise decision management approach includes the decisions in applications and aligns them to a single operational system or function of the business. This leads to lack of scalability, flexibility and analytic components focused on decision.

3. Extending capabilities of existing systems with service-oriented architecture

Service oriented architecture is recognized in the literature by numerous specialists as the best solution for achieving organization agility. Still, beside the benefits, service-oriented architecture leads to a high complexity. Thus, service-oriented architecture must not be seen as a purpose, but rather analyze the opportunity of using it in the organization strategy. Combining service-oriented architecture with existing systems (for example BI, EDM, BPM) may solve integration problems for the many organizations that are still thriving to achieve it.

Even more, in a collaborative environment, due to cultural and linguistic heterogeneity, varied technological and business development of the organizations, designing solutions for informational systems interoperability remains a complex problem. Also, traditional organizations are affected by (Zeng et al., 2009): 1. weak consistency of organization strategies, business processes and technological systems and infrastructure, 2. inflexible and inexact implementation of business processes in the applications systems, 3. existence of large heterogeneity across organization systems and weak adaptability of information architecture, 4. lack of performance analyses and optimization applications for organization networks.

In a collaborative environment technological solutions must allow the integration of systems, business partners and business users and answer to external events (system events and transactions) and internal events (generated by agents and internal systems) that generate frequent changes in the organization (Mircea et al., 2010). As answer to these challenges, the instruments trend (for example event driven BPM, event based BI) is to provide collaborative capabilities (for example process discovery, modeling and optimization) and dynamic capabilities (for example: dynamic process and service flows, directed by business rules) for flexible business processes. Dynamic capabilities provide agility by detecting patterns and fast adaptation of business processes to events and agents (clients, businessmen, analysts and programmers, architects and process analysts).

The problems of integrating the organization architectural paradigms are useful as data warehousing and service-oriented architecture. While service-oriented architecture can be effective on a transactional, data must be integrated to support high-level management decisions. Architectural principles of the two paradigms are not completely compatible. To resolve differences between the two paradigms, practitioners have proposed several alternatives, among which service-oriented business intelligence, event-driven architecture and enterprise services bus.

The existence of service-oriented architecture allows for the management and automation of decision as decision services. The decision services are logical services of SOA that automate and manage highly targeted decisions that are part of organization's day-to-day operation (Bassett, 2007). Decision services implement operational decisions or business policies to help keep the enterprise in synch with market changes (Collard, 2009). The logic of decisions is provided by business rules defined in business rules management systems. The biggest benefits are achieved when they are stored separately in a rule repository and not integrated in applications. The decision logic code is replaced by invoking a decision service with a mechanism to receive the result from business rules management systems. This allows changing the rules without implications on the existing applications and the implementation of business rules can be carried out by business analysts, not programmers.

Developed on a standard service-oriented architecture platform, decision services provide support for making intelligent decisions for business processes managed by business process management systems. Even more, they can be connected to enterprise service bus to support loose-coupling to business processes, become part of complex event processing solution or enhance existing enterprise applications (FICO, 2009). The architecture may integrate decision services developed in other environments that support business intelligence and allow the users of business intelligence systems to perform the required changes. Figure 3 depicts a proposed architecture environment that combines the capabilities of BI, DM, BPM, SOA and other systems in order to achieve organization agility and transit towards intelligent organization. The proposed solution is focused on decisions, which leads to an organization oriented to action, reality and practice.

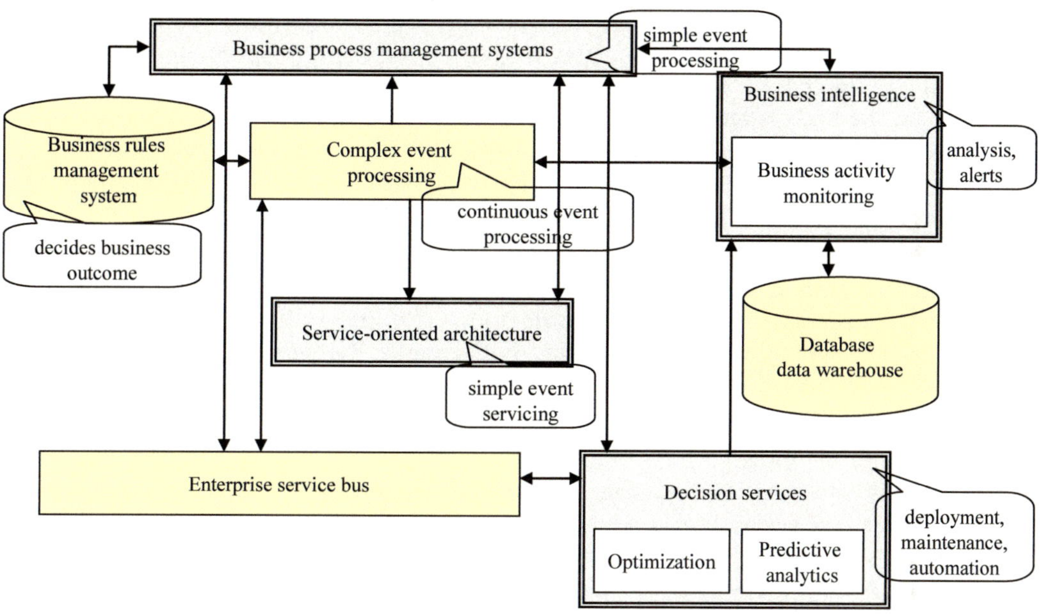

Fig. 3. Agile architecture framework based on SOA, BI, BPM and DM

Within the above architecture, service-oriented architecture facilitates the reuse of decision service through business rules, which can be exposed as web services. *Decision management* services use BRMS rule engines to process the inputs from operational systems through rule services. Additionally, BRMS rule engines process the data from separate data sources and analytic models embedded within rule service in order to return the optimal decision output (Taylor, 2005). SOA allows BPM to separate the business logic from the process logic. Also, it helps improve the availability, information consistency and access to complex and heterogeneous data (operational, transactional, analytical and unstructured information).

The proposed architectural environment ensures the link between analyzing large volumes of heterogeneous and distributed data, making consistent decisions and evaluation of current state by detection and processing of complex events. Business activity monitoring facilitates the control of event in early stages. CEP processes complex events based on business rules and provides simple business events that may be easily manipulated by BPM, BI, SOA and other instruments existing within the organization (Mircea et al., 2010). At the same time, it provides a mechanism for the easy description of events and identification of specific patterns for complex events of the real world.

Three types of decisions to be made based on events are discernible in the context provided by CEP, namely manual, semi-automatic and automatic decisions. For semi-automatic decisions, decision management generates a series of alternatives based on results provided by the CEP engine. CEP solutions generally provide mechanisms to maintain decisions as rules that allow substantiation based on patterns of events. Combined use of BRMS and CEP leads to the finely-tuned orchestration of business information, actions and responses, enabling intelligent and responsive decision automation (IBM, 2010).

The separate placement of the rules and models repository must be observed (from which the rules will be imported to represent entries for decision services), but also the likely presence of one or more databases that, in a software system, are closely related to business rules. In the same time, business rules authoring services (responsible for business definition) are placed in a separate component. In order to facilitate the application maintenance, the knowledge base and inference engine are represented as separate entities (Andreescu & Mircea, 2009). Since rules and policies are those that will change over time, it is not practical to rewrite the code associated with each rule engine each time a new rule appears.

The combination between business rules and web services offers an adequate approach for applications integration and sharing of distributed information. Business rules adoption, together with a service-oriented architecture, allows the integration of strategic corporate applications between multiple business units. For example, the same business logic that has been explicitly defined in a business rules management system may be shared in a service-oriented architecture with other applications that need it. These applications communicate via XML with the business rules services (Holden, 2007).

Business process management helps optimize the business processes within the organization, but does not provide support for processes that extend beyond the organization boundaries. SOA helps solve this issue, ensuring the support required for enterprise-wide BPM (Bajwa et. al, 2008). Also, SOA allows the implementation of BPM to be focused on business processes and not on technological integration requirements (Tibco, n.d.). A service oriented approach allows reuse, governance and offers loose coupling among application modules, especially when considering enterprise-wide BPM. Used together, BPM and SOA allow using services as reusable components that support dynamic business processes (Kamoun, 2007). Business processes based on services can be designed and optimized fast and frequent, as the needs of the organization require.

As for *business intelligence*, service-oriented architecture extends their capabilities, providing support for elimination of redundancy, lack of accuracy, erroneous information (without the use of data warehouses, marts, and stores), as well as a robust architecture for data access and exchange. According to (Hansen, 2008), the best strategy is to apply service-oriented architecture principles to data integration, turning data into a service that is available as logical modules, each with a standards-based interface. Data services help transform data sources into reusable data components, facilitating the access and use and improving data visibility. The study conducted by Ventana, has identified three top benefits SOA brings to business intelligence solutions (Everett, 2006): from business perspective: to make information more broadly available, to be able to respond faster to changing business conditions and to increase the quality and consistency of data; from technological perspective: increased responsiveness to business needs, easier integration of business intelligence with other systems and lower BI life cycle management costs. The benefits of having SOA include flexibility, responsiveness, reusability, ease of connection, cost reduction and agility (IBM, 2007).

Successful creation of new operational and business models involves the existence of an integrated and holistic approach of the information technology, business processes, organization management, structure and culture (Mircea & Andreescu, 2010). The shift to the new model cannot be done only by modernizing the information technology. Service oriented architecture provides a viable and practical approach to exploring services together with business needs (Zhao et al., 2007). The new organizational model tackles both solving current organizations issues and challenges brought by the service oriented collaborative environment.

4. From decision support to decision automation

In practice, the management decision takes two shapes: decision act and decision process. A decision becomes an act when there is a low complexity situation, repeatable and the time required to make the decision is very short - second or minutes. A decision process means a high complexity situation that requires a long time to reach a decision (hours, days or weeks). It can be defined as the sum of phases through which a management decision is prepared, adopted, applied and evaluated.

Decisions represent a critical success factor in reaching organization agility. The complexity of the decision process and frequency of changing rules and business politics imposes the need for automating decisions and decomposing human made strategic decisions into atomic business rules. The business rules must have associated quality attributes in order to be effectively exposed as services in SOA. Access to data is performed through service-oriented architecture, not by duplicating data from one operational system to another.

Decision automation means a series of tools and platforms (figure 4) used to find the model (step 1), model (step 2) and implement (step 3) the decision and define the calculation algorithm. Automated decisions are the result of translating an organization's strategic objectives into tactical business policies and requirements, which can then be implemented as decision logic for use within and across enterprise systems (IBM, 2010). Manual decisions require a human factor (business experts) and they do not allow modeling the decision. They can only be defined in a context and require human experience and judgment.

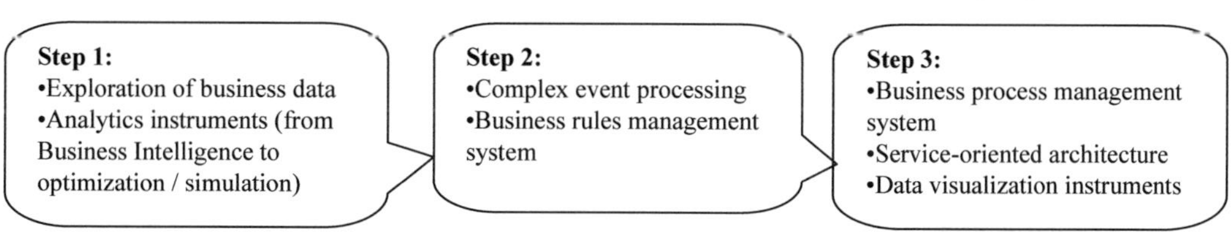

Fig. 4. A range of tools and platforms necessary in decision automation

Step1. In this step informational systems can provide the information about internal and external conditions that might affect the decision. Thus, an analysis can be performed over the organization operations or activities that take place in the business field. Also, informational systems may be used to analyze the external environment in order to identify potential decision situations. Business analytics provide key analytical capabilities that bring additional insight and oversight to improve complex decision-making.

Foundation information can describe economic phenomena, indicating the state or behavior. They transform into potential decision type information, then into effective decision information, indicating changes that must be induced in the behavior or state of the phenomena reflected by the information. When foundation information is about notions, they can be first transformed into phenomena information and then transformed into decision type information. Thus, the information about notions passes into decision type information, indicating the changes that must be induced to the notion, which, in turn, transform into decision type information about phenomena (see figure 5).

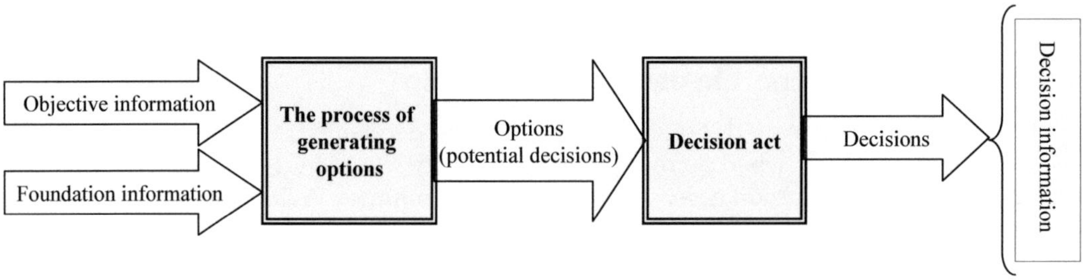

Fig. 5. How an economic decision is made (after Stoica, 2005)

An important factor in the management system is the subjectivity in consuming the information for foundation of intuitive decisions and / or giving an abnormal importance to some information in decision models. The importance of information for a decision may be measured by coefficients of participating in the foundation of the decision. Incomplete consuming of the information - giving a lower importance in making the decision - may lead to underestimating the phenomena effect and unnecessary increase of expenses to reach the goal. On the other hand, if too much importance is given, accomplishing the condition at the level set by the decision will only accomplish a part of the objective because the relation between foundation information and the decision objective is particular and its intensity is given by the dependency between the two economic phenomena or processes. Therefore, we can say that is it important to determine the participation coefficients or information in founding the decision and they must be taken into account when the decision model is built and /or intuitive decisions are made.

Another aspect of the information systems is the uncertainty of information used to substantiate a decision. The uncertainty of information is defined as a difference between the real economic process or phenomena and its representation as information. Generally, uncertainty means a lack of synchronization between the informational representation and the real economic system. Information uncertainty has a direct influence both on shaping the decision objectives and on defining the alternatives to accomplish them. Founding information uncertainty influences the uncertainty of alternatives, leading to increased expenses to reach the goal or insufficient conditions to reach it. Therefore, the uncertainty of information has a special importance in formulation and creation of conditions required to achieve the decision objective, with high influence on the efficiency of informational and management activities. Information uncertainty comes from both the limitations of information gathering process and the way the informational system is organized and functions. From the informational system perspective, information uncertainty is determined by the quality aspects - accuracy and authenticity.

The first stage of model discovery requires tools, processes and techniques for exploration and analyses of business data. (Taylor, 2010) presents the evolution of analytics instruments from Business Intelligence, descriptive analytics, predictive analytics and optimization / simulation, according to the level of complexity. They are used for analyses and description of historical data and trends (descriptive analyses), description and predictions about the future (predictive analyses), finding the best solution for a problem under a set of constraints and a clear objective (optimization). The advanced analytics and analytic modeling capabilities can be incorporated into business intelligence architectures like analytics oriented business intelligence or they can be integrated separately into the enterprise decision management solution.

Step 2. When used together CEP and BRMS provide "always-on" mechanisms for data pattern detection and precise decision automation (IBM, n.d). Decision automation capabilities provided by rules and events may be used for complete automation of interactions, for decisional support or decisional orientation of the human factor. CEP provides a mechanism for easy description of events and identification of patterns of complex events in the real world. CEP solutions generally provide mechanisms for storing decisions as rules that allow substantiation based on event patterns.

Most BRMS products allow or even require the placement rules that will to be executed together into a set of rules (Andreescu & Mircea, 2009). The motivation resides in the need to associate rules governing a particular function of an application. For example, all rules that are related to discounts may be grouped in the set of rules "discount rules". Rules syntax checking includes the possibility to check the syntactic correctness of a rule, in real time and as the rule is introduced into the system. It is obvious that an efficient business rules management process can't be achieved without the use of suitable instruments for this purpose. There are plenty of such instruments on the market, that provide facilities for business rules acquisition and management, each covering a specific area of rules life cycle and addressing to different categories of users. BRMS (Wilson & Stineman, 2010) help automate complex, highly-variable decisions that take place in various stages of a process or separate processes within the organization.

Step 3. Business process management is used to define and orchestrate the various tasks and services that comprise the end-to-end business process (Wilson & Stineman, 2010). In most cases, the BRMS is exposed to business process management through web services that are invoked by the process to make a decision that has direct influence on how the business operates. Beside business process management and service-oriented architecture, visual interpretation of complex relations between multidimensional data with the help of data visualization instruments is a required element in implementation of the decisional model. An integrated solution will provide support for fact-based and data-driven decision making. The decision process will produce information. Without this information and without communicating it through the informational system the decision will have no effects. In all decision models the role of information in the decision making process is essential.

Decision automation largely depends on their typology; decisions may be classified based on: the way they are made (formalized and intuitive decisions), the purpose (process triggers and behavior adjustment decisions), type of decision maker (individual or group decisions), certainty of achieving the goal (certain and uncertain decisions), time frame and implications on the organization (strategic, tactical and operational decisions), frequency (periodic, random and unique decisions). Since decision automation became a feasible solution, organizations must choose what decisions to automate / semi-automate and what decisions should be left to the stakeholders.

Considering the large volume of decisions, high level of repetition and consistency, operational decisions are best suited for automation. Operational decisions are characterized by a large number of rules that change frequently and are hard to manage manually or through traditional approaches, complexity of rules, the need for business experts to understand them, the need for predictive analyses that should be integrated in the decision process, well understood factors, a relatively structured domain. In big organizations, operational decision automation generally becomes more of a survival condition than a need. The correctness and speed of making and implementing these decisions is the foundation for the existence and success of the organization.

Tactical decisions are a candidate for automation if they are complex enough and with a moderate economic impact. Generally, tactical and strategic decisions are made by decision makers and information systems provide the support for founding them. Figure 6 presents simple decisions (low complexity, low value) that are easy to automate, expert decisions (high complexity, high value) that are made with the help of decision support technologies, and between them the manual decisions. The use of operational analytics in the first stage of the decision automating process leads to an increase of the automation area, because of this main reasons (Taylor, 2010): 1. analyses of large amounts of data, finding templates, presentation of results and calculation of the risk an automated decision might have; 2. replacement / extension of personal experience in making a decision with the analyses of historical decisions made in similar cases.

Automation may be applied for information retrieval, integration and analyses, design of decision model, decision selection and /or action implementation (Parasuraman et al., 2000). During the decision model design stage, the decision case may be programmable or non-programmable, or generally structured or unstructured.

Structured decisions (programmable) are the cases where making a decision is based on a predefined procedure. Thus, decisions are structured or programmed by decision procedures or rules developed for them. A structured decision may involve a deterministic or algorithmic decision. In this case the result of the decision can be determined with certainty if a specified sequence of activities is performed (an algorithm). Also, a structured decision may involve a probabilistic decision case, where the probabilities to achieve possible results are known with an admissible margin of error.

Unstructured decisions (non-programmable) involve decision cases where it is not possible or it is undesirable to specify in advance procedures to follow in making the decision. In reality many decision cases are unstructured because they depend on random events or involve unknown factors or relations. At best, many decisional cases are semi-structured. This is why some decision procedures may be predefined but not sufficient to lead to a definitive decision.

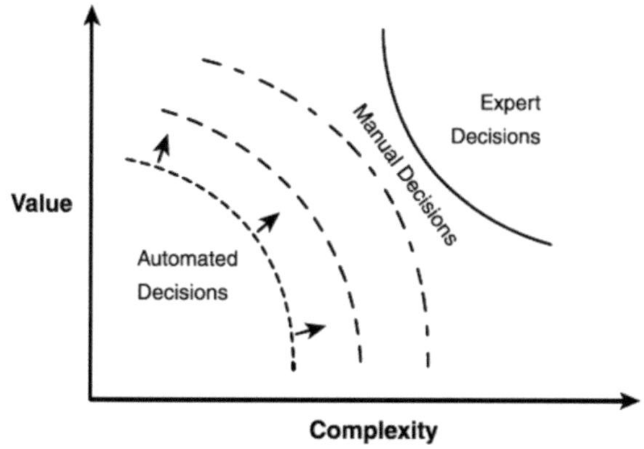

Fig. 6. Operational analytics can increase the range of decision automation (Taylor, 2010)

In order to function efficiently in a contemporary organization, the decision must fulfill some rationality requirements:

a. to have a scientific founding - management personnel must have both the knowledge, methods, techniques and abilities to make decisions as well as the understanding of market economy mechanisms;
b. to be empowered – to be made by the management body that has it as explicit work task;
c. to be integrated, harmonized in the assembly of decisions made or designed to be made – decision integration, both on vertical and horizontal of the management system guarantees the achievement of the unity of decision and action principle;
d. to fit in the optimum time frame for making and implementation – organization management must have a predictive approach;
e. to be clearly formulated – the decision must be clear, concise and state the objective and main operational parameters; in other words, the decision must indicate the objective pursued, the projected actions, allocated resources, the decision maker, the responsible for implementation, where does it apply and the time frame or deadline for implementation.

5. Conclusion

This chapter shows how business intelligence, decision management and service-oriented architecture solutions may be used together in order to create an intelligent organization that draws benefits on both short and medium / long term. The dynamics specific to modern management manifests itself at the level of the informational system, with a high level of perfection, on multiple levels. A major contribution to this is the technological development of the means to process the information. The advantages of the information technology may be capitalized only as long as managers and employees are open to change. The change must be understood as a change of human state of mind in the context of redefining the organizational culture (seen as the sum of values, beliefs, aspirations, expectations and behavior developed in the course of time in each organization, that prevail within the organization and conditions, directly and indirectly, the functionality and performance). Last but not least, we have to take into account the growing role of neo-factors of production in the current socio-economic and political context, among which organizational information and culture are in pole position. Since business intelligence, decision management and service-oriented architecture solutions are merely some of accessible technological panaceas for collecting, transmitting, processing and using the information, the conclusion is that who owns the information and knows how to integrate it into decision making processes in a favorable market context, he shall win. He will be in position to benefit from strategic advantages and have control of the business, capitalizing on economic opportunities through the solutions proposed in this chapter (and not only) … *quod erat demonstrandum.*

6. Acknowledgment

This work was supported by CNCSIS-UEFISCSU, project PN II-RU (PD), "Modern Approaches in Business Intelligence Systems Development for Services Oriented Organizations Management", code 654/2010, contract no. 12/03.08.2010.

7. References

Andreescu, A. & Mircea, M. (2009). Managing Knowledge as Business Rules. *Informatica Economică*, Vol. 13, No. 4, (December, 2009), pp. 63-74, ISSN 1453-1305

Bajwa, I.S.; Kazmi, R.; Mumtaz, S.; Choudhary, M.A. & Naweed, M.S. (2008). SOA and BPM Partnership: A paradigm for Dynamic and Flexible Process and I.T. Management. *World Academy of Science, Engineering and Technology*, Vol. 45, No. 4, (September 2008), pp. 16-22, eISSN 2010-3778

Bassett, G. (2007). Decision Services: Pragmatic Real-Time Analytics. *Information Management Magazine*, No. 42, (December 2007)

Brătianu, C.; Vasilache, S. & Jianu., I. (2006). In search of intelligent organizations. *Management & Marketing*, Vol. 1, No. 4, (December 2006), pp. 71-82, ISSN 1842-0206

Collard, R. (2009). Agile Decision Services: How IBM ILOG's Business Rule Management System helps Organizations Deliver Fast Time to Value for Business and IT, In: *IBM*, 07.10.2011, Available from ftp://public.dhe.ibm.com/common/ssi/ecm/en/wsw14058usen/WSW14058USEN.PDF

Dove, R. (2001). *Response ability: The language, structure, and culture of the agile enterprise*, John Wiley & Sons, ISBN: 978-0-471-35018-7

Everett, D. (2006). Service-Oriented Architecture Can Benefit Business Intelligence, In: *Ventana*, 07.10.2011, Available from http://businessintelligence.com/research/208

Fico (2009). Decide to survive, four imperatives that make better decision management essential in uncertain times, In: *FICO*, 07.10.2011, Available from http://www.fico.com/en/FIResourcesLibrary/Insights_Decide_Survive_2535WP.pdf

Hansen, D. (2008). Demystifying Data Federation for SOA. *SOA Magazine*, No. 22, (September 2008), pp. 1-8

Holden, G. (2007). Reactive and Proactive Business Intelligence, In: *BeyeNETWORK*, 07.10.2011, Available from http://www.b-eye-network.co.uk/view-articles/5899

IBM (2007). Infrastructure Considerations for Service-Oriented Architecture, In: *IBM*, 07.10.2011, Available from http://www-935.ibm.com/services/us/its/pdf/wp_infrastructure-considerations-for-service-oriented-architecture.pdf

IBM (2010). Working smarter through intelligent, responsive decision automation. How the combination of Business Rule Management and Business Event Processing can increase business agility, In: *IBM*, 07.10.2011, Available from http://www.informationweek.com/whitepaper/download/showPDF?articleID=177800015

IBM (n.d.). Decision Management Technologies: Business Rules Management and Business Event Processing, In: *IBM*, 07.10.2011, Available from http://www-01.ibm.com/software/websphere/products/business-rule-management/decision-management/technologies.html

IDC (2008). Improving Organizational Decision-Making Through Pervasive Business Intelligence. The Five Key Factors That Lead to Business Intelligence Diffusion, In: *IDC*, 07.10.2011, Available from http://www.artisconsulting.com/SiteCollectionImages/MSBIC/PervasiveBI-5KeyFactorsforBIDiffusion.pdf

Kamoun, F. (2007). A Roadmap towards the Convergence of Business Process Management and Service Oriented Architecture, In: *Magazine Ubiquity*, 07.10.2011, Available from http://dl.acm.org/citation.cfm?id=1247273

Media (n.d.). The Need for Smart Enough Systems, In: *Media.techtarget.com*, 07.10.2011, Available from http://media.techtarget.com/searchDataManagement/downloads/SmartEnough_ch01.pdf

Mircea, M. & Andreescu, A. (2009). Using Business Rules in Business Intelligence. *Journal of Applied Quantitative Methods*, Vol. 4, No. 3, (September 2009), pp. 382-393, ISSN 1842-4562

Mircea, M. & Andreescu, A.I. (2010). Agile Systems Development for the Management of Service Oriented Organizations, *11th International Conference on Computer Systems and Technologies, CompSysTech'10*, pp. 341-346, ISBN: 978-1-4503-0243-2, ACM PRESS, Sofia, Bulgaria, 17-18 June, 2010

Mircea, M.; Ghilic-Micu, B. & Stoica, M. (2010). Combining Knowledge, Process and Business Intelligence to Delivering Agility in Collaborative Environment, In: *2010 BPM and Workflow Handbook, Spotlight on Business Intelligence*, L. Fischer (Ed.), pp. 99-114, Future Strategies Inc., ISBN-10: 0981987052, ISBN-13: 978-0981987057, Florida, SUA

Morris, H. (2010). Business Analytics and the Path to Better Decisions, In: *IDC*, 07.10.2011, Available from http://fm.sap.com/data/UPLOAD/files/IDC%20White%20Paper%20for%20Launch.pdf

Parasuraman, R.; Sheridan, T. B. & Wickens, C.D. (2000). A model for types and levels of human interaction with automation. *IEEE Transactions on Systems, Man, & Cybernetics*, Vol. 30, No. 3. (May 2000), pp. 286-297, ISSN 1083-4427

Pega (2010). BAA selects Pegasystems to Enable Airport-Collaborative Decision Making Initiative at Heathrow, In: Pegasystems, 07.10.2011, Available from http://www.pega.com/about-us/news-room/press-releases/baa-selects-pegasystems-to-enable-airport-collaborative-decision-m

Stoica, M. (2005). *Sisteme informaţionale economice. Concepte şi studii de caz*, ASE Bucureşti, ISBN 973-594-723-4, Bucharest, Romania

Taylor, J. (2005). Achieving Decision Consistency Across the SOA-Based Enterprise Using Business Rules Management Systems, In: *Web Information Systems Engineering*, M.

Kitsuregawa et al. (Eds), pp. 750-761, Springer-Verlag Berlin Heidelberg, Retrieved from http://www.springerlink.com/content/71n274q38877u962/fulltext.pdf

Taylor, J. (2009). Decision Management Contrasted. *Business Rules Journal*, Vol. 10, No. 9 (September 2009), 07.10.2011, Available from http://www.BRCommunity.com/a2009/b499.html

Taylor, J. (2010). Operational analytics: putting analytics to work in operational systems, In: *BeyeNetwork*, 07.10.2011, Available from http://www.decisionmanagementsolutions.com/attachments/155_BeyeNetwork OperationalAnalyticsResearchReport.pdf

Tapscott, D. & Tapscott, B. (2010). Collaborative Decision Management, In: *Purus*, 07.10.2011, Available from http://www.purustech.com/wp-content/uploads/2011/01/cdmwhitepaper.pdf

TIBCO (n.d.). Business Process Management on an SOA Foundation: A Unified Framework for Process Design and Deployment, In: *TIBCO*, 07.10.2011, Available from www.tibco.com/software/soa/

T-systems (2010). More transparency, security and efficiency, In: *T-systems*, 07.10.2011, Available from http://www.t-systems.com/tsip/en/167410/home/solutions/vertical-solutions/overview-travel-transport-logistics/airport-management-services

Ventana (2006). Business Intelligence Meets Business Process Management. Powerful technologies can work in tandem to drive successful operation. *Ventana Research.* 07.10.2011, Available from http://www.techsoli.com/pages/resources/pdfs/Ventana-BI_and_BPM.pdf

Vesset, D.; Fleming, M.; Morris, H.; Hendrick, S.; McDonough, B.; Feldman, S.; Traudt, E.; Olofson, C. & Webster, M. (2010). Worldwide Decision Management Software 2010–2014 Forecast: A Fast-Growing Opportunity to Drive the Intelligent Economy, In: *IDC*, 07.10.2011, Available from http://www.idc.com/research/viewdocsynopsis.jsp?containerId=226244

Vickoff, J-P. (2007). Agile Enterprise Architecture. Architecture of a generation of high-performance enterprises. In: *Entreprise-Agile.com*, 07.10.2011, Available from http://www.entreprise-agile.com/en/PumaIntroEN.pdf

Wang, N. & Lee, V. (2011). An Integrated BPM-SOA Framework for Agile Enterprises. In N.T. Nguyen, C. G. Kim and A. Janiak (Eds.), *ACIIDS 2011*, pp. 557-566, Berlin Heidelberg, Springer-Verlag

Wilson, C. & Stineman, B. (2010). Confused about when to use BRMS, BEP, BA and BPM? Understanding what decision management has to do with business process management, In: *IBM News*, 07.10.2011, Available from http://www-01.ibm.com/software/solutions/soa/newsletter/nov10/brms.html

Yu, D. & Zheng, S. (2011). Towards Adaptive Decision Support Systems: A Service-oriented Approach. *Advances in Information Sciences and Service Sciences*, Vol. 3, No. 7, (August 2011), pp. 26-34

Zeng, S.; Huang, S. & Fan, Y. (2009). Service-Oriented Enterprise Network Performance Analysis. *Tsinghua Science and Technology*, Vol. 14, No. 4, (August 2009), pp. 492-503, ISSN 1007-0214

Zhao, J. L.; Tanniru, M. & Zhang L.J. (2007). Services computing as the foundation of enterprise agility: Overview of recent advances and introduction to the special issue. *Information Systems Frontiers*, Vol. 9, No. 1, (February 2007), pp. 1-8, ISSN 1572-9419

3

Adding Semantics to Business Intelligence: Towards a Smarter Generation of Analytical Tools

Denilson Sell[1,2,3], Dhiogo Cardoso da Silva[2], Fernando Benedet Ghisi[1,2], Márcio Napoli[1,2] and José Leomar Todesco[1,2]
[1]Instituto Stela,
[2]UFSC – Universidade Federal de Santa Catarina,
[3]UDESC – Universidade do Estado de Santa Catarina,
Brazil

1. Introduction

Fierce competition in the digital economy and increasing volume of available data are forcing organizations to find efficient ways to gain valuable information and knowledge to improve the efficiency of their business processes. Business Intelligence (BI) solutions offer the means to transform data to information and derive knowledge through analytical tools in order to support decision making. Analytical tools should support decision makers to find information quickly and enable them to make well-informed decisions.

Despite the importance of analytical tools to organizations, there are challenges that should be tackled in order to leverage the impact of those tools in the decision making process. These challenges include difficulties to extend those tools according to the business requirements, no support to analyze and interpret data and lack of flexibility to customize information presentation according to users' profile.

We argue that these issues are due to the lack of integration of business' semantics into the foundations of analytical tools. Our approach applies ontologies on the description of business rules, information sources and business concepts in order to support semantic-analytical functionalities that extend traditional OLAP operations. Such approach enables developers to customize BI solutions according to organizations' specific analytical requirements and allows developers to align BI solutions to the latest business analytic requirements. In addition, this approach made it possible to offer novel approaches to guide decision makers on the analysis of their business, including recommendation according to users' profile, a question answering approach to access business data and automatic generation of text summaries based on OLAP cubes.

The improvements on knowledge engineering and related technologies offer new approaches to tackle traditional issues in the context of information management. In this chapter, we describe how Semantic Web technologies and business semantics were applied on the conception of an architecture for analytical tools. Our ultimate goals are to contribute to a new generation of analytical tools that may drive decision makers from the investigation of their business to the implementation of actions according to insights obtained in their investigations.

The Semantic Business Intelligence (SBI) architecture presented in this chapter incorporates many features that distinguish it from the existing information management solutions and research. Our work aims at enabling the integration of business semantics, heterogeneous data sources, and knowledge engineering tools in order to support a smarter decision making.

In the first section, we present how we design our architecture and present each of its modules. We subscribe to semantic technologies to define an integrated architecture for analytical tools. The architecture is supported by business semantics that, in turn, are applied to contextualize the organizations' resources (i.e. logic, data sources and services). The architecture comprises a set of modules to support automated recommendation of analysis, inferences, relations and services according to the context of an analysis. Semantic web services and logic reasoning are applied to support flexible extension of exploratory functionalities and powerful analyses. Information about these analyses and actions made by decision makers are captured to form an important repository of explicit knowledge that can support future decisions.

We present how the potentialities of our architecture were used to leverage analytical tools in different scenarios. On top of our architecture, we developed different strategies in order to provide an intelligent behavior in the analytical environment.

One of the applications described in this chapter shows how we are applying natural language to support decision making and information retrieval. The need to obtain and use knowledge to support the decision making motivates the convergence of the new generations of Business Intelligence (BI) solutions with the Knowledge Engineering tools. Despite application of semantic technologies and methods of knowledge representation, BI research still lacks the use of natural language to conduct analysis. The metaphor of information searching conjectured on the Semantic Web is becoming a trend in the area of BI. Thus, we describe how our architecture made it possible the gathering of strategic information from corporate data sources driven by means of the semantic interpretation of natural language questions. This approach brings to the BI area of the discipline of Question Answering (QA) and the Semantic Web formalisms through an interdisciplinary approach. Some resources of knowledge representation, such as ontology, inference rules, idiomatic patterns and heuristics aid the architecture's functional modules with the interpretation of question and the return of the OLAP cube.

An analytical interface was constructed to allow the entry of questions in the Portuguese language, the interaction with the decision maker to resolve ambiguities and the visualizing hypercubes. As well as the way millions of users search for information on the Web, this research provides an innovative method to aid in the decision making process.

2. The semantic business intelligence architecture

The SBI architecture comprehends a set of loosely-coupled modules that are illustrated in the Fig. 1. The SBI ontologies comprise business semantics and describe the relationship among such semantics, BI terminology, operational semantics, and data sources.

SBI ontologies are used by the QueryManager to parse analytical tools and data requests, and to execute such requests on heterogeneous data sources, enabling the combination of unstructured and structured data on the very same analysis. The OntologyManager is the module that provides access to SBI ontologies. Such module relies on a Reasoner to support on-the-fly and batch based inferences over business semantics. These inferences make semantic driven slice and drill based on business rules possible.

In the following sections, we describe in details the SBI ontologies and its modules.

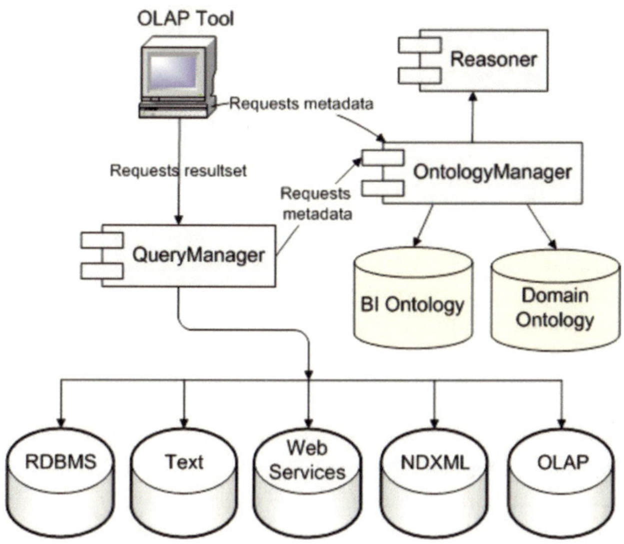

Fig. 1. Illustration of SBI main components

2.1 The SBI ontologies

In our approach, we use ontologies to capture business semantics and to define the necessary knowledge models for generating flexible and exploratory functionalities in analytical tools. In current version, the SBI ontologies have a version modeled in RDF (Lassila & Swick, 2004) and OWL (McGuinnes & Harmelen, 2004). In the following sections, we introduce the domain and the BI ontologies.

2.1.1 The domain ontology

The domain ontology supplies the business terminology used to enable data sources annotation. Therefore, users will be able to explore information repositories by using business concepts instead of technical descriptions. Also, the relations, rules, and logical expressions described in the domain ontology will support semantic drill and slice, query definition, and extraction of further details from data presented by analytical tools.

All required inferences to extend the analytical functionalities are supported by business rules and expressions represented in the domain ontology. Domain specific relations and rules can be defined to slice and drill OLAP cubes. The Listing 1 below defines the *Alumni* rule that infers institutions in which students have completed their degree. A new relation called *isAlumni* between *Person* class and *Institution* class is inferred by this business rule.

Person(?p) ∧ Degree(?d) ∧ Institution(?i) ∧
hasDegree(?p, ?d) ∧ hasInstituion(?d, ?i) ∧
isCompleted(?d, 'yes') → isAlumni (?p, ?i)

Listing 1. The Alumni rule: former student of an institution

The notation above states that a person (?p) is a former student of an institution (?i) when she has completed her degree (?d). Business rules, such as alumni depicted in listing 1 are represented in the domain ontology using SWRL (Horrocks et al., 2004).

The mapping of domain concepts to the BI ontology is described in the next sections.

2.1.2 The BI ontology

The BI ontology models the concepts used to describe how the data is organized in data sources and to map such data to the concepts described in the domain ontology. These definitions are used to: a) support inferences using the domain ontology to extend query results; b) support the presentation of query results using business terminology; c) provide an abstraction of data sources to guide the interaction of decision maker on the exploration of organizations' information sources. The main concepts related to business intelligence are modeled in the BI ontology. Fig. 2 shows its main constructors.

As depicted in Figure 2, the BI ontology maps OLAP concepts used by analytical tools to guide decision makers on analysis definitions and to provide semantic drill and slice operations. The information source concepts are used to represent data source structures and to map those structures to domain concepts represented in the domain ontology. The Table 1 presents more details about BI ontology concepts.

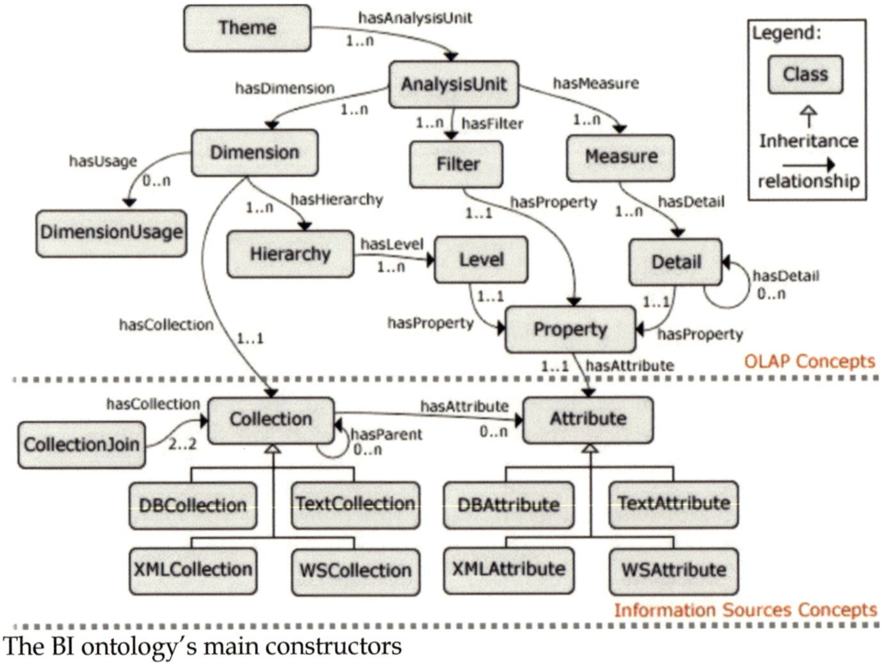

Fig. 2. The BI ontology's main constructors

Concept	Description
Theme	A Theme represents documents, fact and dimension tables associated with a business process (e.g. *R&D*)
AnalysisUnit	It defines fact tables and document collections related to a specific subject of a theme. In the R&D theme, for instance, one can find AnalysisUnits such as *School dropout*. An AnalysisUnit may have several dimensions and measures
Measure	This concept is used to represent quantitative values, aggregations or summarizations related to AnalysisUnit content (e.g. *Number of students*)
Filter	Filters are dimension attributes that could be applied to slice and dice data related to an AnalysisUnit (e.g. Students age, gender and so on)
Dimension	It describes analysis units dimensions. Dimensions can have many hierarchies and properties (e.g. *State*)
Hierarchy	This concept describes dimension hierarchies. Each hierarchy is composed of one or more levels (e.g. *City, State, and Country*).
Level	It represents a hierarchy level that is used on drill-up and drill-down operations.
Detail	It describes how an analysis unit can be detailed or presented in its atomic level. (e.g. *name, e-mail*).
Property	Property identifies the terminology used to present an information unit. It also maps instances of the attribute concept to instances of detail, filter, level, and measure concepts.
DimensionUsage	It describes how data collections are linked to analysis units.
Collection	This concept represents a data collection or a data provider and describes how these data sources relate to the concepts represented in the domain ontology.
CollectionJoin	It describes how a collection can be joined to another collection. It also identifies which properties and operations are used to join two collections.
Attribute	It corresponds to items contained in collections such as table fields, XML elements, entities extracted from documents, or spreadsheet columns. The Attribute concept also associates these elements with slots of concepts represented in the domain ontology.

Table 1. Description of BI ontology concepts

2.2 SBI Functional modules

SBI ontologies are used by functional modules to support analytical tools on the localization and exploration of data sources.

The QueryManager supports analytical tools by providing a transparent access to heterogeneous data sources and data providers based on a XML-based protocol. It enables the combination of query results from structured or non-structured data sources, independently of their localization. The QueryManager hides data sources complexities from analytical tools. Requests of analytical tools are translated by QueryManager in queries that are processed on corresponding data sources. Analysis definitions (i.e. analysis units, filters, measures and so on) from analytical tools are received and translated in an XML message. The OntologyManager retrieves the information required from the BI ontology.

The OntologyManager component is responsible for manipulating the BI ontology and retrieving the necessary information to support the formulation of data requests. It retrieves details about data collections such as table names, their field definitions and their relationships from concepts defined in the domain ontology.

QueryManager performs intersections or unions between heterogeneous repositories by using common attributes of each result set returned by drivers. For instance, an inverted index structure is used just to find the papers ids produced by students, and these ids are used to join with other information about such students stored in a data mart. In this example, one can summarize the number of students by department that has written papers that mention the term "semantic web."

In our approach, for each type of data repository or data provider, we create a different driver to handle specific issues of that data source. For instance, in the textual driver, a set of algorithms were used for data indexing and retrieval (Beppler et al., 2005), while the RDBMS driver uses JDBC driver to access relational data bases.

2.2.1 Reasoning

Since SBI ontologies are described in formal language that enables the explicitation of business rules and the definition of axioms for specifying relationships between concepts, Semantic slice and drill are made possible by the architecture ontologies in which relations and rules are applied to filter or expand the results of queries relying on synonyms, hyponyms, and other relations specified in the SBI ontologies.

In order to infer new knowledge or, more precisely, to provide new ways to decision makers explore their data, we have integrated OntologyManager to Jena (McBride, 2002) and Pellet (Sirin et al., 2007).

In our approach, all results of inferences are stored in a data mart, more specifically in a star schema called *Triple Model*. The Triple Model is used as an extension of a dimensional model and its tables can be connected to the remaining tables in data marts. In this strategy, semantic inferences occur in batch as the traditional ETL processing. So, besides the strategic information available in the dimensional model, the OLAP tools can also access the inferred conclusions from business rules processed over the data stored in data marts.

The triple model is composed of an associative table, called *Triple Fact*, and a dimension, called *Inferred Predicate*. The triple fact table is responsible for storing inferred information that describes different relationships between two dimensions. The relationships inferred from business rules are stored in the inferred predicate dimension. In the triple model the reference of each dimension represents a subject or an object similarly to RDF statements.

Figure 3 illustrates the Triple Model integrated to a star schema. In this example, the DI_PERSON dimension is a subject and the DI_INSTITUTION dimension is an object of a statement stored in the triple fact table. Such relation has been inferred from business rules such as *works in*, *graduated in* and *alumnus of* described in the domain ontology.

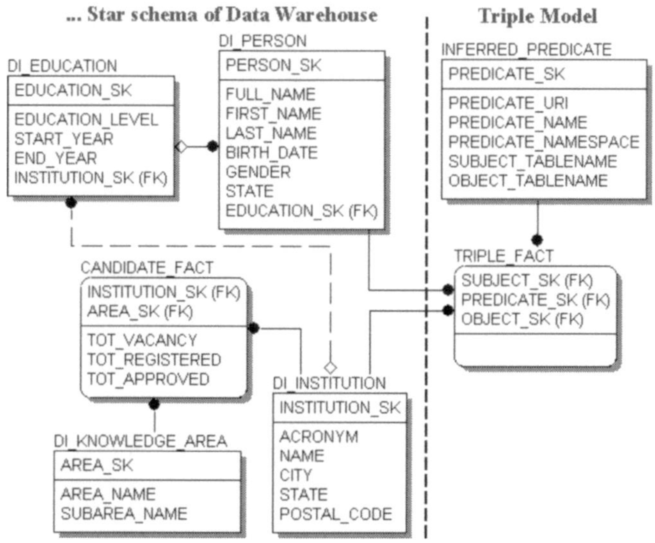

Fig. 3. The triple model and its integration with star schema

Our approach enables the creation of multiples associations between dimensions based on business rules. For instance, at any time, a knowledge engineer can add new business rules in the domain ontology to define new kinds of relationships between people and institutions.

The reasoning process is performed by a Reasoner such as Pellet (Sirin et al., 2007) integrated to the OntologyManager, as follows:

1. The OntologyManager imports the domain ontology model and its business rules. In this step, in the R&D scenario described before all classes, properties, axioms and business rules are brought to the OntologyManager work area.
2. The OntologyManager reads all BI ontology instances used to map the domain ontology to data sources. In this step, each concept defined in the R&D domain ontology will be associated to the Collection class' instances. In addition, all domain properties will be associated to instances of Attribute and CollectionJoin classes.
3. The OntologyManager retrieves the necessary data to create the domain ontology instances. The query is guided by the mapping between business concepts and data sources defined in the BI ontology.
4. New instances of domain ontology are created by OntologyManager based on the information retrieved in the last step.
5. Once created the instances, the reasoner is invoked to perform inferences based on business rules defined in the domain ontology. In this step, the *isAlumni* rule shown in the Listing 1 is applied.
6. At last, the OntologyManager stores inferred concepts from domain ontology into triple model. The new inferred concepts are saved into the inferred predicate dimension and the new relations between two dimensions are stored in the *Triple Fact*.

The inferred information stored in the Triple Model may be accessed by analytical tools to offer decision makers the possibility to slice, dice and drill over data sources by applying business rules defined in the domain ontology.

3. SBI and its question answering approach to support decision making

It is true that the simplicity of current Web search continuously contributes to the growth of its popularity. The ease of use in these search interfaces allows that by informing a few words in free text one can find almost any type of content so fast and ubiquitous. For its intuitive and natural way of providing access to information for people of virtually all ages, the same metaphor of Web search should be considered for the next generation of BI solutions. Such trend for the future of BI takes into account its proximity to resources and services of the Web, both in the use of heterogeneous sources as in the way of finding information (Bohringer et al., 2010; Howson, 2007).

The combination between the new research on BI and aspirations of the Semantic Web is focus of study that can be addressed further. To meet different stakeholders, it is necessary to the analytical tools rely on strategies for the representation of business knowledge and mechanisms the make it possible the use of that knowledge in the exploration of data sources. Just as the Semantic Web provides agile ways and navigation interfaces based on high semantic expressiveness to locate relevant content on the Internet, BI architectures must also make use of semantic to support the analytical processing. However, BI solutions lack the use of effective methods of exploration of content such as those already used by the billions of current Web users, yet without losing the potential conjectured by the Semantic Web (SmallTree, 2006).

Analytical tools usually require long and expensive training sessions due to: a) the potential number of users and time needed to train those users; b) the complexity of the tools; and c) the skills of each user. To reduce these costs, the use of natural language is considered one of the most appropriate and feasible strategy (Conlon et al., 2004). Therefore, the ability to express information needs through natural language should be introduced in the new BI architectures and is the goal of this work.

In this research, analysis submitted to the organization' data sources, instead of being guided through the conventional OLAP operations, are carried out through the semantic interpretation of a question expressed in natural language. That is, we provide access to OLAP cubes through questions stated by users in their language, in which the concepts and terminology of the business are expressed descriptively and independent of specific formalisms.

Unlike the strategies of searches driven by keywords, we apply an approach based on knowledge engineering methods and Question Answering (QA) techniques (Katz et al., 2001; Kauffman & Bernstein, 2007; Lopez et al., 2007). This approach is characterized by adopting more significant use of natural language or questions for returning a data cube that may have the information required by the decision maker.

3.1 Question answering support

The processing of natural language questions is performed by the modules of the architecture in three main steps: 1) a step associated with the construction and maintenance of the model and knowledge base, which is essential for the subsequent steps, 2) a second step related to the interpretation of the question and its formalization in a structure that represents its meaning, 3) a third and final step responsible for returning an OLAP cube.

The first step occurs prior to the decision-making process and should be performed regularly according to the evolution of the domain ontology and to the growth and changes in data sources of the organization. It aims at preparing the ontology and knowledge base used both in the process of analysis and interpretation of the question formulated by decision makers. In the second step, the question reported in natural language is analyzed and processed by a set of methods and technologies that rely on the semantic context defined by the organization's domain ontology. Here, some QA tasks are applied to the interpretation of questions aimed at translating the natural language in a formal language. This formal representation of the resulting question has the definition of quantitative measures, descriptive groupings and filters for the execution of OLAP operations (e.g. drill-down, roll-up, slice, dice, etc.). Once the query is built and formalized, in the last step the information request is performed on the data sources in order to answer the question.

The following figure shows the arrangement of the complementary elements of the SBI architecture as follows: processes and techniques - representing the tasks, techniques, procedures and processes performed by functional modules of the architecture, inputs and outputs - input data and results of the processes and techniques; functional modules - architecture subsystems or components developed by third parties that have some peculiarities in the roles they play and, repositories and data sources - include repositories of ontologies, models and knowledge base, configuration items and also the data sources.

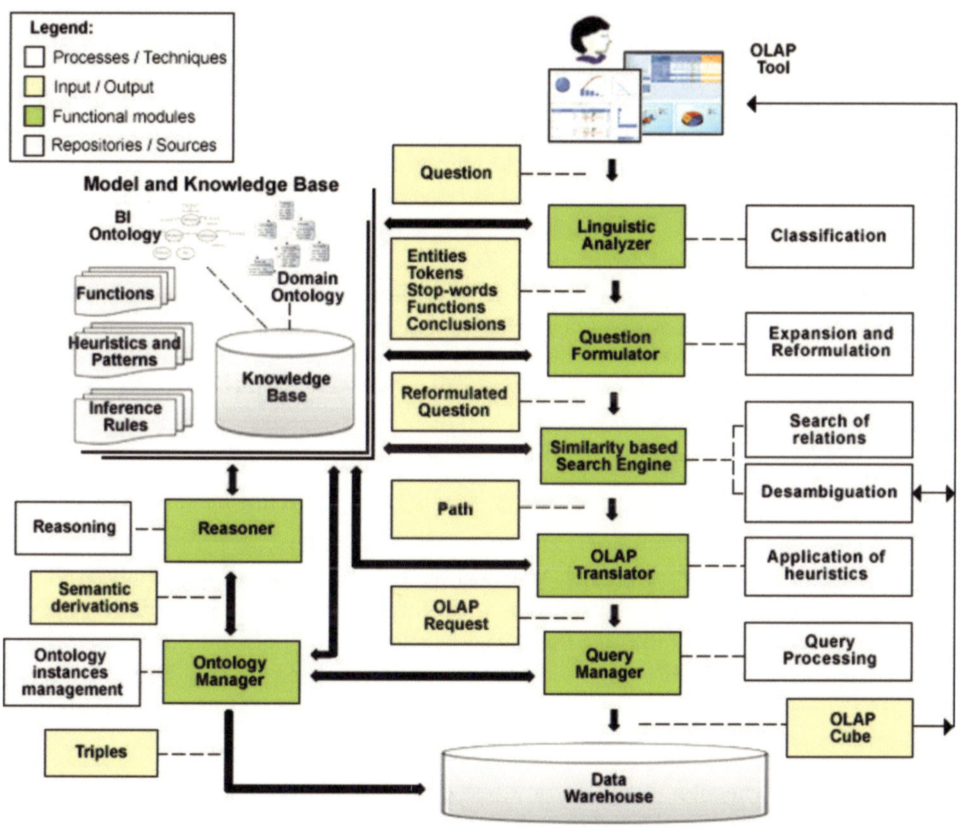

Fig. 4. Schematic view of QA modules

In a nutshell, the question after being informed by the decision maker in the OLAP module is assessed by the Linguistic Analyzer. This module classifies all the elements of the question as specific concepts, such as textual entities, stop-words, functions and other specific classifications reported below. From the classification of the tokens of the question, the module applies query expansion and reformulation techniques to detail and expand the question proposed originally. Based on the reformulated question, the module Similarity Search Engine tries to find relationships between concepts and entities in the question by searching the domain ontology. Once discovered the relationships between concepts in domain ontology, the OLAP Translator converts the question in a formal request, including the definitions of filters, projections and quantitative measures to be considered in the query. Then, the Query Manager performs the request on the DW to return the OLAP cube with the strategic information to decision makers. The semantic inferences performed in the process can be combined with information from the DW. The Knowledge Base serves as a central element in which the functional modules rely to complete each task. The following section describes the main SBI modules.

3.1.1 Knowledge base

The Knowledge Base comprises knowledge resources required in all the steps from the interpretation of decision makers' questions to the queries execution on data sources, as follows:

a. Knowledge Base and Inference Rules - repository formed by the instances of the Domain Ontology, the organization's business rules and instances of the BI Ontology.
b. Functions – consist of functions that must be associated with some specifics words used by the decision maker and with some domain ontology concept. A function assigns one output (e.g. dates, numbers, etc.) to each specific input text. For instance, the words *Today, Tomorrow, Yesterday* could produce a date as output in order to create an instance of the ontology class called *Time*.
c. Heuristics and Linguistic patterns – it represents regular expressions, lexical and syntax patterns, heuristics designed by a specialist according to the language and the distance between words. These resources must be stored on the Knowledge Base in order to support OLAP Translator identification of measures, projections and filters in the question introduced by the decision maker.

3.1.2 Linguistic analyzer

In the first step, the Linguistic Analyzer proceeds with a lexical, syntactic and semantic analysis of the question. The Linguistic Analyzer executes a set of tasks to analyze all textual elements contained in the question in order to classify them and get information needed to interpret the question formulated by the decision maker. As Question Answering systems, this work applies classification tasks and also introduces particular kind of classes to interpret the question and to support OLAP queries on Data Marts. These classes are grouped in six categories as shown in the Table 2.

Linguistic Analyzer executes some techniques of natural language processing to classify question terms, namely, POS-Tagging, Lemmatization, Stemming, Named-Entity Recognition, Co-reference and search into dictionaries.

Classification or feature	Description
Stop-word	Words with a high frequency in texts and usually with no relevant content in traditional QA works. In this research, the stop-words are particularly useful in the identification of OLAP constructors, such as measures, projections and filters.
Position or Order	It identifies the position or order of each token in the question. This information is used to recognize the linguistic patterns and heuristics, in which are stored on the Knowledge Base, according to distances between classes of words.
Function	When a term is associated with a function defined in the Model and Knowledge Base.
Conclusion of inference rule	When the term is contained in a conclusion of inference rules. (e.g. the concept "Alumni" presented in the listing 1)
Entity or Domain concept	It represents a domain ontology concept, such as, a class, a relationship, a property or an instance of a class.
Unknown token	Tokens not classified by the Linguistic Analyzer.

Table 2. Classifications and features of textual terms

During the classification task, some textual elements can generate ambiguities. That is, Linguistic Analyzer can identify two or more classifications for the same term. Likewise, a term classified as a domain concept may represent a class, a property of class, a relationship or an instance of class as well. These ambiguities are not resolved by Linguistic Analyzer and they are processed and eliminated by the module called Similarity Search Engine afterward.

After of the classification tasks, the question can be reformulated and expanded by the Query Formulator module presented below.

The Linguistic Analyzer performs a process with emphasis on each specific term of the question without focusing on the semantic relations among words. The Similarity Search Engine, by verifying the relationship between words and contextual information, can reduce or even eliminate the ambiguities. Therefore, the disambiguation is delayed and performed only once through the Similarity Search Engine. In practice, the Linguistic Analyzer identifies an ambiguity in the question when:

1. The textual entity is an instance of two or more classes of the domain ontology.
2. The textual entity is a class and is similar to two or more classes of the ontology. This case appears when two or more classes have the same name or synonyms in common and are mentioned in the question.
3. The textual entity is a relationship or property and belongs to two or more classes involved in the question. This case is commonly found as the concepts can share the same properties or have equivalent relationships in a given context.
4. The textual entity has similarity between classes, instances, properties or relationships of the domain ontology. This occurs when the term has the same textual description of a class, also a property or a class instance.

Once executed the process of linguistic analysis and obtained ratings for all the terms, the question can be reformulated or expanded through the Question Formulation module described in the following section.

3.1.3 Question formulation

Once the lexical-syntactic and semantic classifications are obtained from the elements of the text, the question is reformulated. This process aims to enrich and expand the original question in order to generate all the information necessary to create the OLAP request later. The reformulation process is also a characteristic of Question Answering systems. It comes to finding important facts related to the domain that have been omitted or reported differently by the user and that should be incorporated to complete and formalize the question. This work uses two types of reformulation that can be applied successively. The first strategy is based on the class hierarchy and synonymy relations and the other applies a rule-based inference approach.

The synonyms as well as superclasses and subclasses of the entities found in the question are necessary in the question reformulation because there are different ways to express the same request through natural language. Thus, the terminology that was reported in a given question can be exchanged for another that is more adherent or closer to the domain context.

The reformulation by inference rules is applied when the query terms are classified by Linguistic Analyzer as being *conclusions of inference rules*. At this stage the facts contained in the conclusions or consequents of the rules are used to reformulate the question. That is, the triple of concepts () that is in the consequent of a rule is used to replace the term classified as conclusion of the inference rule by Linguistic Analyzer.

From the classification and reformulation tasks made by linguistic analysis and query reformulation respectively, the next step is finding which path or set of relationships between concepts that best fit the question. This goal is accomplished by the module Similarity Search Engine that is described in the following section.

3.1.4 Similarity search engine

Based on the question reformulated in the previous step, the Similarity Search Engine performs a search on the model of the domain ontology to discover which path is closer to the context of the question. The textual elements used in the question are confronted with the concepts represented in the domain ontology by Similarity Search Engine in order to check the best path (or the only set of relationships between concepts used in the question) that can resolve the question. Therefore, the concepts of the domain ontology, along with their synonyms and hierarchies are used to evaluate possible alternatives to extract the information required by the decision maker.

The Similarity Search Engine analyses the sequence of concepts or classes (vertices) mentioned in the question and their relationships (edges) in the domain ontology. The Similarity Search Engine chooses the best way to solve the question considering all the terminology given by the decision maker. In this research, as applied by Lopez et al. (2007), the best path is characterized as the one that presents the greatest amount of relevant concepts and relationships according to the terms informed in the question.

The Similarity Search Engine may find more than one possible path to tackle the question. Thus, in addition to previously scenarios of ambiguities solved by Linguistic analysis, this module is responsible for resolving ambiguities among candidate paths. Therefore, two types of disambiguation are likely to be made by the Search Engine Similarity: disambiguation of concepts (i.e. considering classes and properties ambiguous) and disambiguation of paths (i.e. considering relationships ambiguous).

Both disambiguation processes may require decision maker intervention to complete. According to the user's choice in this process, the question is refined iteratively until there is no doubt the meaning of the elements mentioned in the question and about which is the best path to solve the information request.

The Similarity Search Engine, as its name indicates, performs searches on the domain ontology, relying on synonyms, class hierarchy, and other types of relationships defined in the ontology. Searches are supported by a textual index in order to speed up the path retrieval. After discovering the best path as well as the concepts related to the terms mentioned in the information request, the final query can be built and processed on the data sources. The work of translating the best path in a request to explore the Data Warehouse is performed by the OLAP translator described in the next section.

3.1.5 OLAP translator

The OLAP Translator, based on the path chosen in the last step, identifies the measures, groupings, filters and connections between concepts that may be applied in order to extract the data needed to solve the information request. a translation of the best path found by the search engines to an OLAP request, which will be performed later by DW Query Manager module.

Measures represent numerical measurements (sum, average, minimum, maximum, etc.) on a particular domain concept. Measures classified by the OLAP Translator are associated with facts and attributes of dimensions defined in the dimensional model. The concepts translated as groupings identify the descriptive information used to group or categorize the measures in the queries. These concepts should generally be associated with attributes of the DW dimensions and are the classes' properties.

When the concepts are translated as filters, the values related to these concepts are used as selection criteria in the OLAP request. Usually, the element of the question is translated as a filter when referring to a class instance, or when a value of a property identifier (name, initials, date, etc.) is given.

In addition to the measures, grouping and filters, the OLAP translator should also define how should be represented the relationships of these items. Each relationship between the classes denotes joins or connections that must be used between objects of the data sources. All relationships between concepts, including those resulting from the inference rules in the process of reformulation, must be presented on the result produced by the Similarity Search Engine.

In order to make the translation of the path in a query, OLAP translator uses a set of patterns and heuristics based on distance or position between the concepts of the question and stop-words. Although the words classified as stop-words are ignored by most IR systems, they are essential at this stage of translation. Generally, research on QA applies stop-words to classify the type of question and also to identify the syntactic pattern to answer it correctly. In this work, the stop-words also help the discovery of the elements of OLAP query, such as measures, grouping, filters and joins.

All syntactic patterns and heuristics along with a list of stop-words used by OLAP translator must be configured according to the language in the knowledge base. This setting allows regular expressions and criteria based on the position or distance between tokens and stop-words to be used by the OLAP Translator. Thus, there is greater flexibility in the recognition of elements of the query according to the idiomatic patterns or writing mode of decision makers.

To perform the translation and to set standards in the Knowledge Base, this paper adopts three types of stop-words arranged as shown in Table 3.

Stop-word type	Query element	Description
Quantification	Measure	Stop-words that deal with numeric values summarization or calculations and data quantification. Expressions such as *how many*, *how much*, and its variants, such as *which and total* are considered.
Projection	Grouping	Stop-words used to categorize or group content typically descriptive, without the need to quantify them, such as the dimension attributes. Examples are the stop-words *by*, *for*, *as*, *grouped by*, *second*, etc., on questions like "how many students by age and by city study in the South?".
Selection	Filter	Stop-words used to filter a data set - relational operators such as *above*, *equal to*, *greater than*, *less than*, etc. - and even logical (logical operators), such as *AND* and *OR*. Example of question with relational stop-words: "How many specialists *over* 40 years and *below* 50 years have published articles in 2010?". Example of question with logical stop-words: "How many teachers *and* students study Human Physiology *or* Occupational Health?".

Table 3. Types of stop-words for OLAP translation

3.1.6 Applying SBI on science and technology management

This section shows an application of the architecture for the Science & Technology management, including the evaluation and analysis of intellectual productions and academic and professional activities of researchers, teachers and students of Federal University of Santa Catarina (UFSC). The sample data used as data source comes from the Lattes Institutional Platform[1] (LIP), from UFSC. Thus, the main concepts and terminology - such as person, degree, educational institution, academic and professional activity, production, among others - are modeled in the domain ontology.

[1] Lattes Institutional Platform - http://lattes.ufsc.br

From the domain ontology, a structure similar to a textual index was created so that the best path can be located by Similarity Search Engine. As in IR models, this index forms a matrix with the set of terms and their synonyms extracted from each path of the domain ontology, as shown below in Figure 5.

Figure 5 illustrates how some of the paths (concepts and relationships of domain ontology) are organized into an IR boolean model. This type of model is adopted in the construction of the architecture to demonstrate how the paths can be discovered in practice. However, the architecture does not limit the adoption of other forms and structures for organizing and finding paths. Thus, other mechanisms and methods can be used to support the construction of the Knowledge Base module, in order to fulfill the goal of the Similarity Search Engine module.

Due to the presence of synonyms and class hierarchies in the matrix of paths, the process of reformulation based on class hierarchy and synonyms is treated at once by Similarity Search Engine. Thus, the Similarity Search Engine developed also acts as a reformulator, except for cases of reformulation by inference rules.

Based on the matrix created, the question, after passing through the stages of linguistic analysis and reformulation, is used as input vector by Similarity Search Engine to perform a search. Here, all stop-words are ignored and only they are exploited later by OLAP Translator.

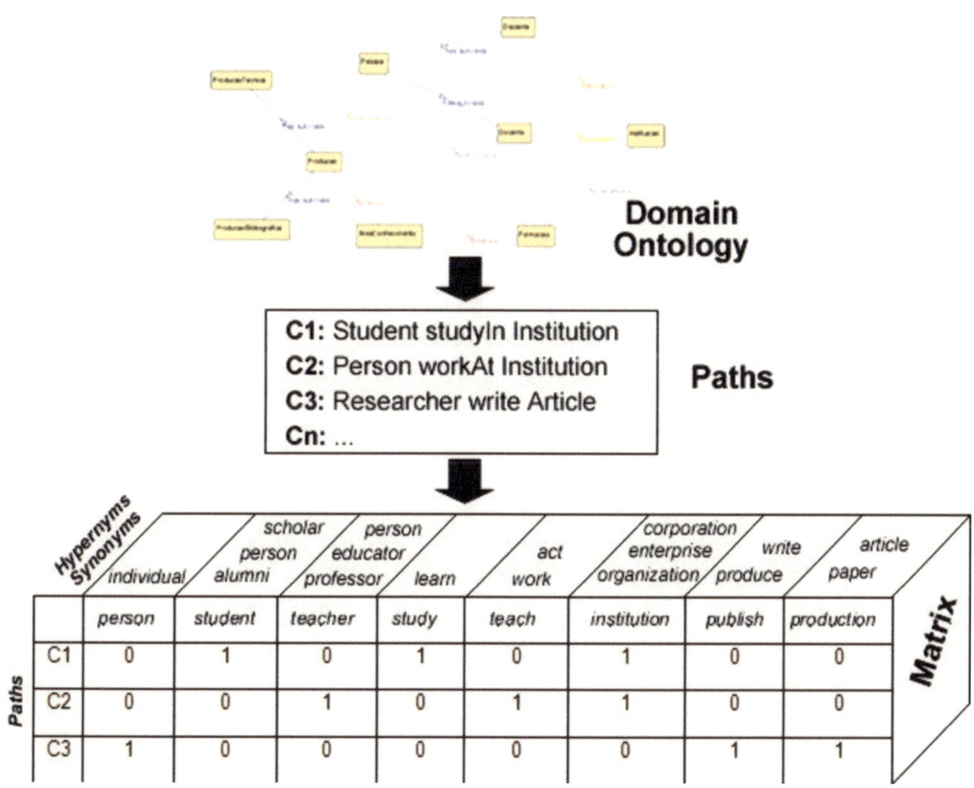

Fig. 5. Illustration of the matrix of paths obtained from the domain ontology

Based on the domain context and in the language used, Knowledge Base should also contain the knowledge of how to identify the elements of OLAP queries, such as measures, groupings, filters and joins. This knowledge is formed by the lexical-syntactical patterns, the relative positions of the query terms and by heuristics based on the types of stop-words previously described in Table 3. The representations of these patterns and heuristics are formalized in the Knowledge Base by means of regular expressions that match the positions of recognized entities of the question and the types of stop-words. The patterns and heuristics used by the OLAP Translator module are detailed in Table 4 according to each element of the associated query (measure, grouping, filter or join).

Nº	Query element	Description of the pattern or heuristic
1	Measure	All terms classified as classes and class properties positioned immediately to the right of stop-words of quantification, which are followed or not by the tokens AND or OR, are classified as measures.
2	Grouping	All terms classified as classes and class properties located to the right of stop-words of projection, which are followed or not by the tokens AND or OR, are classified as groupings.
3	Grouping	The direct classes of terms classified as instances of classes are always used as groupings.
4	Filter	All terms classified as instances of classes or identified as class property values are used as filters. Note: If the term is not to the right of a stop-word of selection (see classification in the Table 4.), the criterion of equality (=) is used to filter the content; otherwise, the stop-word of selection will be considered. The tokens AND and OR present between the values of properties or instances of classes are used as logical operators of the filter criteria.
5	Join or relationship	All relationships between the concepts of domain ontology are used as joins or relationships in OLAP request. In own BI Ontology mapping, these relationships must be matched with joints or relationship between the tables and dimensions in the query.

Table 4. Patterns and heuristics used to formulate OLAP requests

To clarify how heuristics and patterns are applied, consider the following question: *"How many students*[1]*, by gender*[2] *and academic training*[2]*, study*[5] *at CSE*[3,4] *or CFH*[3,4]*?"*. The terms superscript numbers refer to the number of the respective pattern or heuristics in Table 3. In this example, the term "students" refers to the class "Student" and is classified as a measure because it has proximity to the right of the stop-word *How many* (by Rule 1). The attribute set in the BI Ontology as a standard measure of the class "*Student*" should be used to quantify the information in the query. Yet, the two terms "*gender*" and "*academic training*", although with the same numbering (number 2), the first represents a property of the class "*Person*" and the second represents directly the class "*Degree*" on the domain ontology.

In this case, the first (the term "*gender*") is used directly as a grouping, the second (the term "*education*"), the default attribute of the class "*Education*" is defined as a group that should be applied. The terms "CSE" and "CFH", instances of the class *"Instituition"* in this example, are used as filters (by rule 4) and also presented in the return of the query (by rule 3). Again, the attributes of the class *"Instituition"* as defined in the BI Ontology should be used as a filter and aggregate by the OLAP translator. As the terms "CSE" and "CFH" are not involved with the stop-words selection, the equality criterion (=) is used in the filter of data comparison in the query. The logical OR is used to build the filter criteria, because the token "or" is informed in the answer between the terms in question. Finally, by applying the pattern number 5 in Table 4, the word *"study"*, which symbolizes a relationship in the domain ontology, is used as a join for the OLAP request. Once this relationship is given in the path returned by the Similarity Search Engines, the OLAP Translator recognizes that the term *"study"* relate the concepts *"Person"* and *"Instituition"* in this example.

As the dictionary that helps the terms classification, the stop-words are arranged according to their type in the Knowledge Base. These stop-words are defined according to the previous classification given in Table 4. Then the set of stop-words used for the examples of questions in the S&T scenario is shown in Table 5.

Quantification	Projection	Selection			
		Relational Operator		Logic Operator	
		Term	Operator	Term	Operator
how many; how much; amount of; which the amount of; total of; number of	by; according to; grouped by; as;	Above, greater than	>	and	AND
		Below; less than;	<		
		From	≥	or	OR
		Equal to	=		

Table 5. List of stop-words used according to type

The stop-words applied as filters are related one by one with a specific operator. For example, the stop-word formed by the tokens "Above" is associated to the operator ">" the stop-word "From" and its variants are associated with operator "≥", and so on. Others stop-words could be added as required and organization´s standard writing. However, this work is limited to the set of stop-words shown in Table 5.

The following figure shows a prototype analytical tool to support users interaction on top of SBI QA components, where the domain ontology of S&T is illustrated along with the regions of the input query and display the results. This figure shows an example of a question in the context of S&T with its own answer. The steps to obtain the OLAP cube from this question are detailed below.

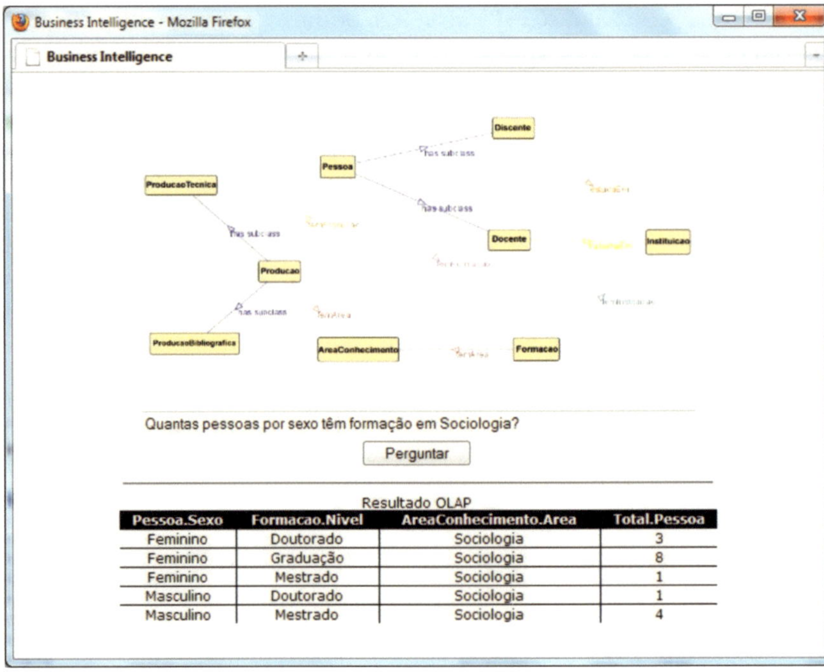

Fig. 6. Illustration of a prototype analytical interface

The question "How many people by gender have education in Sociology?" shown in Figure 6, is a simple example which presents no ambiguities, conclusions of inference rules and no functions. That is, only the class properties, classes and their relationships domain ontology of S&T are involved in the question.

Initially, this question, after being informed at the interface must go through the process of lexical analysis, syntax and semantics of Linguistic Analyzer. By consulting the dictionary and concepts of the S&T domain ontology, the Linguistic Analyzer determines the classification of each term in question, in this case: *"How many"* (stop-word of quantification); *"people"* (*Person* class); *"by"* (stop-word of projection); *"gender"* (class property of *Person*); *"have"* (*token* not recognized); *"education"* (*Education* class); *"in"* (*token* not recognized) and; *"Sociology"* (instance of *KnowledgeArea* class). The *tokens* not recognized (on this example, *have* and *in)* are not between the dictionary terms and classes of the ontology, so, do not have defined classification.

Before finding the best path based on the domain ontology, the Query Reformulation module in this example replace the instance "Sociology" by respectively class *"KnowledgeArea"*. Since the question does not have classified terms as conclusions of rules there is not reformulation based on inference rules. However, for this example reformulation by using synonyms and class hierarchies are performed. This reformulation is performed by Similarity Search Engine that performs also the role of the Query Reformulation module.

The reformulated question that should be used as input to the search for Similarity Search Engine show only the terms: *"Person gender have education in KnowledgeArea"*. Note that some terms classified as stop-words were ignored in the input vector for the search. The terms *have* and *in*, even not being classified, are used in the search, and special characters are removed.

Only the paths that have the highest number of concepts identified from the input vector are returned by the Similarity Search Engines. So, the best path the S&T domain ontology in this example is (represented in N3): *(Person hasEducation Education) - (Education hasArea KnowledgeArea)*. Note that the other paths, such as those formed by only a single vertex (*Persona; Education or KnowledgeArea)* and those formed by the triple; (*Person hasEducation Education)* or (*Education hasArea KnowledgeArea)* should not return in the search. Thus, in this case a single path is obtained without the need for participation of the decision maker for the disambiguation of entities and paths. Otherwise, the alternatives found are presented to the user that should pick one of the options.

With the best path defined, the set of patterns and heuristics presented in Table 4 is applied by the OLAP translator. Thus, from the classified elements and the types of stop-words, the generated OLAP request has as a measure: the *Person* class, as grouping: the property *gender* and the classes *Education* and *KnowledgeArea*, and as a filter: the term *Sociology*, instance of the *KnowledgeArea* class. The relationships (*hasEducation* and *hasArea*) are also translated in the request as relationships (joins) that connect the concepts of the domain.

Thus, Query Manager works with the Ontology Manager module to assemble and execute the derived query with the dimensions or fact tables associated with the concepts identified in the last step (in this case, *Person, gender, hasEducation, Education, hasArea and KnowledgeArea*). The instances of BI Ontology that map these concepts to the DW structure are retrieved by Ontology Manager. After locating these instances, the Ontology Manager tells to the Query Manager the dimensions, attributes, fact tables and how they are interconnected to create the SQL query.

As seen, the properties of classes are most often associated with the dimension attributes in the BI Ontology. However, only one property (*gender* property from *Person* class) were reported and recognized in question. According to the translation from OLAP Translator, a default attribute must be set to measure, group or filter for the class. Thus, when a class has no property explicitly informed the default attribute is set to the BI Ontology to be used in the query.

Thus, considering the configuration of the BI Ontology and the question of this example, the dimension attribute *PERSON_SK* from *DI_PERSON* dimension is used as the standard measure and corresponding to the *Person* class. Since the class *Education*, which corresponds in BI Ontology to *DI_EDUCATION* dimension, has as attribute group *EDUCATION_LEVEL*. Finally, the *KnowledgeArea* class has as group and also filter *AREA_NAME* attribute from *DI_KNOWLEDGE_AREA* dimension.

To find out the joins that link the dimensions *DI_PERSON*, *DI_EDUCATION* and *DI_KNOWLEDGE_AREA* in the query, Query Manager uses the relationships *hasEducation* and *hasArea* obtained from the identified path. Also, Query Manager gets the information through the BI Ontology through Ontology Manager to identify the joins between the tables. This information configured in the BI Ontology indicates which attributes of the dimensions is used to describe the join and the type of join (*inner join*, *left join*, etc.). Finally, the resulting SQL query is performed by Query Manager in order to answers the question.

4. Conclusion

The improvements on knowledge engineering and related technologies offer new approaches to tackle traditional issues in the context of BI and analytical processing. Just as the Semantic Web provides agile ways and navigation interfaces based on high semantic expressiveness to locate relevant content on the Internet, BI architectures should also make use of semantic to support the analytical processing. However, BI solutions lack the use of effective methods of exploration of content such as those already used by the billions of current Web users, yet without losing the potential conjectured by the Semantic Web.

SBI architecture was applied in several e-gov projects and is used, for instance, by three ministries in Brazil (education, environmental, and S&T) to publish data to the Brazilian society and to support internal decision making. The results of the application of our approach in such projects shown that an approach based on ontologies make it easier to handle business rules changes and to offer a more tailored vision over public data on several BI projects.

Our approach incorporates many features that distinguish it from the existing BI solutions and research. The present work aims at enabling the integration of business semantics, heterogeneous data sources, natural language and analytical tools in order to support a smarter decision making.

SBI proved, through case studies, to be a liable alternative for the construction of flexible BI solutions aligned to business logic and decision maker's needs. The following features were made possible by our approach:

- Information is presented to the users using their own vocabulary and in logical views that make it easier to locate information and understand their meaning;
- The definition of business concepts is used to present structured and non-structured data sources available in the organization or remotely;
- Structured and non-structured data can be combined in the same analysis;
- Knowledge and business rules definitions can be altered any time, providing more flexibility to align analytical tools to the latest business rules.
- New possibilities of slice and drill were made possible by combing business semantics and two different reasoning strategies.
- Strategic information is gathered from corporate data sources driven by means of the semantic interpretation of natural language questions.
- Information is summarized by means of textual summaries.

We described how SBI combines knowledge engineering and Question Answering techniques through an interdisciplinary approach. Ontologies, inference rules, idiomatic patterns and heuristics are applied by the architecture's modules on the interpretation of question expressed by decision makers and to produce OLAP cubes to provide all the data needed by SBI users.

Future work comprehends capture of further information about decision makers' interactions with the available functionalities of semantic analytical tools. We are investigating how to extract rules from this information aiming to support automatic analysis of the business and recommendation of actions.

5. References

Beppler, F. D., Todesco, J. L., Gonçalves, A. L., Sell, D., Morales, A. B. T., & Pacheco, R. C. S. (2005). Uma Arquitetura para Recuperação de Informação Aplicada ao Processo de Cooperação Universidade-Empresa, *Proceedings of the KM BRASIL*, São Paulo, November 2005.

Böhringer, M., Gluchowski, P., Kurze, C., & Schieder, C. A. (2010). Business Intelligence Perspective on the Future Internet, *Proceedings of the Sixteenth Americas Conference on Information Systems*, Lima, Peru, August 2010.

Conlon, S.J., Conlon, J.R., & James, T.L. (2004). The economics of natural language interfaces: natural language processing technology as a scarce resource. *Decision Support Systems*, Vol. 38, No. 1, October 2004.

Horrocks, I., Patel-Schneider, P. F., Boley, H., Tabet, S., Grosof, B., & Dean., M. (21 May 2004). SWRL: A Semantic Web Rule Language Combining OWL and RuleML, In: *W3C Member Submission*, 22 May 2010, Available from: <http://www.w3.org/Submission/SWRL>.

Howson, C. (2007). *Successful Business Intelligence: Secrets to Making BI a Killer App*, McGraw-Hill, 978-0071498517, New York.

Katz, B., Lin, J., & Felshin, S. (2001). Gathering Knowledge for a Question Answering System from Heterogeneous Information Sources, *Proceedings of the ACL Workshop on Human Language Technology and Knowledge Management*, Toulouse, France, July 2001.

Kaufmann, E., & Bernstein, A. (2007). How Useful Are Natural Language Interfaces to the Semantic Web for Casual End-Users?, *Proceedings of the 6 th International Semantic Web Conference and 2nd Asia Semantic Web Conference*, Busan, Korea, November 2007.

Lassila, O, & Swick, R. R. (February 2004). RDF/XML Syntax Specification (Revised), In: *W3C Recommendation*, 22 May 2010, Available from: <http://www.w3.org/TR/REC-rdf-syntax/>.

Lopez, V., Uren, V., Motta, E., & Pasin, M. (2007). AquaLog: An ontology-driven question answering system for organizational semantic intranets. *Web Semantics: Science, Services and Agents on the World Wide Web*, Vol. 5, No. 2, (June 2007), pp. (72-105), 1570-8268.

McBride, B. (2002). Jena: A Semantic Web Toolkit. *Internet Computing, IEEE*, Vol. 6, No. 6, (Nov/Dec, 2002), pp. (55-59), 1089-7801.

McGuinness, D. L., & Harmelen, F. v. (February 2004). OWL Web Ontology Language Overview, In: *W3C Recommendation*, 22 May 2010, Available from: <http://www.w3.org/TR/owl-features/>.

Sell, D., Silva, D. C., Beppler, F. D., Napoli, M., Ghisi, F. B., Pacheco, R. C. S., & Todesco, J. L. (2008). SBI: a semantic framework to support business intelligence, *Proceedings of the First International Workshop on Ontology-supported Business Intelligence*, 978-1-60558-219-1, Karlsruhe, Germany, October 2008.

Sirin, E., Parsia, B., Grau, B. C., Kalyanpur, A., & Katz, Y. (2007). Pellet: A Practical OWL-DL Reasoner. *Web Semantics: Science, Services and Agents on the World Wide Web*, Vol. 5, No. 2, (June 2007), pp. (51-53), 1570-8268.

Smalltree, H. (June 2006). Business intelligence search: Five myths, In: *SearchBusinessAnalytics.com*, 17 August 2010, Available from: <http://searchbusinessanalytics.techtarget.com/news/1507286/Business-intelligence-search-Five-myths >.

4

Towards Business Intelligence over Unified Structured and Unstructured Data Using XML

Zhen Hua Liu and Vishu Krishnamurthy
Oracle University,
USA

1. Introduction

Traditional data warehousing has been very successful in helping business enterprises to make intelligent decisions through declarative analysis of large amount of structured data stored in a relational database. However, not all enterprise data naturally fit into a relational model. Within an enterprise, there are huge amount of unstructured data, such as document content, emails, spreadsheets, that do not have a fixed schema, or have a very sparse or loose schema that cannot be effectively modeled using relational model. Yet, like relational data, unstructured data record many useful facts that are equally essential and important to be analyzed by businesses to make intelligent decisions. In this chapter, we propose an XML-enabled RDBMS that uses XML as the underlying logical data model to uniformly represent both well-structured relational data, semi-structured and unstructured data in building an enterprise data warehouse that is able to store and analyze any data regardless of existence of schema or not. We show how XQuery used in SQL/XML as a declarative language to do data query, analysis and transformation over both structured data and unstructured content in the data warehouse. We present the rationale for using XML as the logical data model for unified data warehouse query, XML extended inverted text index to integrate structured data query and context aware full text search for unstructured content so as to support efficient data analysis over large volume of structured and unstructured data. We argue that the technical approach of using XML to unify both structured and unstructured data in a warehouse has the potential to push business intelligence over all enterprise data to a new era.

2. Concept of a data warehouse

Inductive reasoning refers to human arriving at a conclusion based on their observations. The inductive reasoning is a bottom up process where a general conclusion is reached from many instances observed and analyzed. (Myers,1986) Data Warehouse and decision support capabilities in modern database management system (DBMS) reflect the human inductive reasoning process. Data Warehouse (DWH) and decision support system (DSS), typically based on an RDBMS, involve extraction of operational data from business activities, transformation of the operational data, and loading of the results conforming to a fixed relational data model into a DWH store. Sophisticated data transformation, analysis, and mining can then be applied to a DWH to derive useful conclusions that assist businesses in making intelligent decisions. Such evidence based decision-making process achieved through DWH is generally accepted as standard business intelligence practices in Enterprises.

To achieve the goal of business intelligence, the design of DWH in DBMS must address the following requirements that are different from operational data store in Online Transaction Processing (OLTP) environment: Data Heterogeneity, Data Extraction and Batch Loading, Large Data Volumes, and Declarative Ad-Hoc Query Performance.

Data Heterogeneity: since DWH store loads data from different operational store, therefore, it is likely that data may not be as homogeneous as operational store is. That is, data may not have well-defined common schema or may not have schema at all. The general trend is that unstructured data content and semi-structured data are more common than well-structured data to process and to query.

Data Extraction and Batch Load: building decision support system involves extraction of data from various operational stores and bulk loading of them into a central DWH store. This is known as ETL (ExTract Load) process. Data transformation is applied during ETL process to convert data from different operational stores into canonical form. To handle large data volume, tables can be partitioned and managed by several data server instances in a clustered environment. Query can use table partition criteria as selection qualification to work on different partitions of data. Data in DWH is typically partitioned based on certain criteria, such as timestamp based range partition criteria or hash partition based on record key or hybrid combination of the two. Such partition scheme facilitates life cycle management of data and enables query parallelism.

Large Data Volume: Given the fast growing of memory core, it is reasonable to assume that operational data are able to all fit in memory such that in memory database processing becomes very attractive to overcome the gap between disk I/O speed and CPU speed. However, the amount of data for DWH store shall never be assumed to fit in main memory. Therefore, DWH design must take into consideration of selecting data layout to be disk I/O friendly. For example, design favoring small number of sequential large I/O requests generally delivers better performance than that of large number of random small I/O requests. Consequently, DWH design usually lays out data in a way to be optimized for large number of read requests instead of laying out data to be optimized for a large number of random frequent data modification requests.

Declarative Ad-hoc Query Performance: declarative query is an attractive property for DBMS so that users can declaratively specify what they want to ask instead of procedurally programming the system on how to obtain the answer. Declarative query language processing with superior performance is critical for the success of DBMS. For operational store, the supported operations over data are usually pre-determined, therefore, the data query and modification requests have deterministic patterns. Operational store query is typically point query using id lookup that selects small amount of data using simple query criteria. However for DWH environment, the query requests are ad-hoc and exploring in nature. The query pattern is less predictive than that of operational store. DWH Query typically involves processing large amount of data to get summarized report to facilitate decision-making process or to mine data to derive insightful conclusion based on statistical analysis. So DWH query can be long running compared with short running point query in operational store.

3. Data warehouse in SQL/RDBMS – its success and limitations

Based on a strong foundation in relational model and algebra (Codd, 1970), relational database management system (RDBMS) is a great success. The practical realization of relational model using Entity/Relationship (E/R) design (Chen,1975) greatly facilitates users to model real world objects into entities with relationships so that they can be managed by RDBMS and queried or modified declaratively using SQL. RDBMS has been very successful in supporting On Line Transaction Processing (OLTP) workloads. Following the success of OLTP, businesses have successfully built DWH using RDBMS to make intelligent business decisions. The strength of DWH using SQL and RDBMS is described in section 3.1.

3.1 Strength of current DWH practices with SQL and RDBMS

3.1.1 Well-defined relational model for structured data

E/R design models structured data objects, that is, objects having well-defined schema, very well. Objects are decomposed into entities (tables) with primitive attributes (columns). Hierarchical tree shaped objects are modeled by one-to-one and one-to-many relationships among entities via primary and foreign key relationships among tables. Graphical objects are modeled by many-to-many relationships among entities via intermediate key mapping tables. Many-to-many relationship enables construction of objects with different hierarchies. Given that data is frequently updated in OLTP workload, high degree of data normalization provides good update performance because same data is not duplicatively stored so that data update occurs only in one place.

DWH schema design in RDBMS follows the same E/R design principle. The common practice is to use star schema where there is a fact table with a set of dimension tables. An example is shown in Tables 1,2,3,4,5 below. Fact table records business transactions. A fact record is a WWWW tuple (Who purchased What,Where and When). In the example below, Table 1 is a Fact table, while Tables 2-1,2,3,4,5 are dimension tables containing Customer, Item, Store and Date dimensions respectively. There is a primary key on id column in each dimension table. The id column of a dimension table is referred as *dimension id*. The dimension id is also stored in the fact table. There is a foreign-key and primary-key relationship between each column of fact table that stores the dimension id and its corresponding referencing dimension table. In addition, for each dimension table, there are *dimensional columns* that specify composite values for that dimension. DWH SQL query involves joins among fact table and multiple dimension tables shown as Query 1. The WHERE clause of DWH SQL query may use combinations of multiple predicates on dimensional values and thus is ad-hoc in nature.

CustomerId	ItemId	StoreId	DateId	QuantitySold	Description
1454	1456	123	13579	2	<sale_comment> This is sold via special summer sale promotion program at the store. The promotion program is conducted along with the independence celebration event in the city. </sale_comment>

Table 1. Transaction fact table

CustomerId	CustomerName
1454	John Smith

Table 2. Customers dimension table

ItemId	ItemName	ItemPrice	ItemCategoryCode
1456	T.V	$250.32	Electronic

Table 3. Items dmension table

DateId	Date	Month	Year
13579	4	July	2004

Table 4. Dates dimension table

StoreId	StoreName	StoreZipCode
123	Eletronic-Supply	45789

Table 5. Stores dimension table

```
SELECT StoreId, count(*)
FROM TransactionFact f, Customers c, Items i, Dates d, Stores s
WHERE f.CustomerId = c.CustomerId AND f.ItemId = i.ItemId AND f.StoreId = s.StoreId AND
f.DateId = d.DateId AND i.ItemName = 'TV' AND s.StoreZipCode >= 45000 and
s.StoreZipCode <= 46000 AND i.ItemPrice < 300 AND d.Year between 2003 and 2005
GROUP BY StoreId
```

Query 1. SQL on Star Schema

3.1.2 Declarative SQL language with high performing SQL engines

SQL is powerful enough to express analytical queries declaratively. Beyond basic conventional aggregation functions, such as sum() and avg(), contemporary RDBMS supports data mining capabilities as built-in functions so that statistical analysis of data can be done declaratively (Milenova et al., 2005). Through database extensibility work from Object Relational DBMS (Stonebraker et al.,1998), user defined aggregation functions and table functions are supported by contemporary RDBMS so that customized analytical logic over virtual table row sources can be integrated into the SQL engine.

DWH has promoted fruitful research results and industrial practices in the past three decades resulting in RDBMSs with well-engineered optimizers and executors to support DSS type of SQL query workload. Advanced algebraic query transformation based on mathematical property of relational set algebra (Seshadri et al., 1996), sophisticated statistics gathering and dynamic sampling techniques, parallel query execution infrastructure (DeWitt & Gray 1992) are well-developed compile time and execution time techniques to speed up SQL query for DWH workloads. Furthermore, the recent trend of hardware acceleration to speed up query execution is a new direction in greatly improving SQL query performance.

3.1.3 I/O friendly bitmap join index structures

The logical query plan of Query 1 on star-schema consists of three phases. The first phase is to probe each Dimension table to find a set of dimension ids given the dimension value.

Then use resulting dimension ids to find a set of row ids of the rows in Fact table that have foreign key value matching the dimension ids using primary key and foreign key relationship between the Fact table and each Dimension table. The *row id* (RID) in RDBMS represents a physical locator to a row, which is typically composed of file id, page number and slot number of a page where the row resides on a page. The second phase is to perform set intersection of the set of RIDs of the Fact table to get a common set of RIDs that satisfy all the AND qualifications in the where clause. The third phase is to use RIDs from second phase to probe the Fact table to do further processing, such as Group By and Aggregation. This phase may involve probing Dimension tables again using dimension ids from the Fact table row to obtain dimension column values if the query selects dimension column value.

Given that a Dimension table is typically small enough to fit in memory, table scans can be used to find a set of dimension ids given a dimension value. However, finding the set of RIDs of the Fact table having these dimension ids via table scan of Fact table yields poor performance due to the large size of the Fact table. The first attempt to improve the performance is to leverage B+ tree index on foreign key columns of Fact table containing dimension ids so that RIDs of the Fact table can be found via B+ tree index access. However, B+ tree index results in many random I/O requests. Excessive seeks followed by small reads after each seek is not I/O friendly.

To resolve B+ tree index performance problem, Bitmap Join Index (O'Neil & Graefe, 1995) can be created between the foreign key column of the Fact table containing the dimension ids and its referencing dimension id column of the Dimension table. In bitmap join index, each row is given a *row ordinal position* (ROP). The bitmap join index maps a dimension value of the Dimension table to a bitmap representing ROPs of the fact table that having that dimension value. Bitmap can be compressed so that small amount of I/O is needed to load all the relevant bitmaps into memory. During second phase, set intersection using bitmaps of ROPs can be executed much more efficiently than that of using RIDs. At the end of second phase, ROPs are converted into RIDs for further processing.

3.1.4 I/O Friendly columnar storage

Columnar storage (Stonebraker et al., 2005) for DWH is an I/O friendly approach to store data in columnar fashion in order to avoid unnecessary disk I/O to read data that is not needed by the query. Furthermore, when all values of a column are stored together, it is more amenable to data compression that reduces amount of I/O and facilitates query processing strategies that directly operate on compressed columnar data (Abadi et al., 2008). We will explore this further in section 5.

3.2 Limitations of current DWH practices with SQL and RDBMS

3.2.1 Limited capability of handling unstructured data

Unlike structured data that has a static schema that fit into the relational model, we define *unstructured data* to represent loosely structured data, arbitrarily structured data, or data with high degree of schema variability. Such data do not fit into the structured relational model. For data having highly varying schema, fitting it into relational model requires constant schema evolution which is not a scalable and maintainable solution. It is more natural to model such data as semi-structured data or as a string of attribute-value pairs.

Without a schema, such semi-structured data can only be stored in LOB (CLOB or BLOB) columns in an RDBMS. Data without conforming to a rigid schema is increasingly becoming common in enterprises. Like structured data, there is valuable information embedded inside unstructured data that can help business enterprise to make better decision. Users are looking to store and query unstructured data without defining a schema first. This exposes a limitation of relational model that requires data to have schema before they are storable and queryable.

3.2.2 Limited queriability of unstructured data

While unstructured data could be stored as LOBs in the RDBMS, there is effectively no means to query the data inside these lobs. Popular RDBMSs have been extended to support Full-text functionality that can be exercised through SQL. Therefore, text in these lobs could be queried using Full-text search. For example, in the transaction Fact table, there is a description column that records the comments of each purchase transaction. Users can query transaction comments using text CONTAINS() function that does keyword search as shown in Query 2. Users can create an inverted text index on description column of the fact table to speed up CONTAINS() function. Organization of inverted text index follows the traditional Information Retrieval (IR) technique (Salton & McGill, 1983) where a posting list is created for each keyword. Given a keyword, the posting list identifies a set of DOCIDs (Zobel & Moffat, 2006). The DOCID is the same as that of ROP, which is a simple integer based sequence number in contrast with RID which is concatenated raw bytes from different components. It identifies the row of the Fact table that has the keyword in the description LOB column.

```
SELECT StoreId, count(*)
FROM TransactionFact f, Customers c, Items i, Dates d, Stores s
WHERE f.CustomerId = c.CustomerId AND f.ItemId = i.ItemId AND f.StoreId = s.StoreId AND
f.DateId = d.DateId AND i.ItemName = 'TV' AND s.StoreZipCode >= 45000 and
s.StoreZipCode <= 46000 AND i.ItemPrice < 300 AND d.Year between 2003 and 2005 AND
CONTAINS(description, 'promotion')
GROUP BY StoreId
```

Query 2. SQL on Star-Schema with Text Search

However, traditional IR (Salton & McGill, 1983) keyword based full text search is restricted to text content search only, it doesn't address querying structured data with text search, nor does it address the capability of providing context aware text search (Yates & Navarro 1996). There is no support for efficiently querying structure and content together. We will explore and resolve this limitation in section 4 and section 5 using XML data model and XML extended text index.

3.2.3 Lack of query optimizer and engine that is able to optimize both structured and unstructured data query

Consider how Query 2, which consists of both structured data query and unstructured content search via CONTAINS() function, is processed in RDBMS, Contemporary processing strategy optimizes and executes the query in two parts. One part is the structured query processing as described in for Query 1 to get a set of RIDs of the fact table.

The other part is unstructured text content search query processing that gets a set of DOCIDs of the fact table rows whose description column containing the search keyword '*promotion*'. Given a keyword, inverted text index returns a set of DOCIDs containing the keyword. The set of DOCIDs is then mapped to set of RIDs. Then these two sets of RIDs are intersected to get common RIDs of fact table. Note the inverted text index stores DOCIDs instead of RIDs in its posting list because DOCIDs are more amenable for delta compression to achieve very compact posting list size and thus reducing I/O traffic (Zobel & Moffat,2006). This two-part processing strategy is rooted in different indexing and query processing strategies in relational and IR approaches. However, the two-part processing strategy does not deliver ideal performance for queries spanning both structured data and unstructured data. We shall present a better strategy for handling such queries in section 5.

4. Using XML data model in a data warehouse for both structured and unstructured data

4.1 Why XML data model in DBMS ?

Paper (Stonebraker & Hellerstein 2005) reveals the evolution of data models in database community starting with the hierarchical model, then network, relational, object, object-relational, leading up to the XML data model. The criticism on XML data model is that it appears to date back to the hierarchical model that is well supported in IMS systems. Indeed XML is a tree-based model forming single hierarchy and thus is not adequate to handle multiple hierarchies. For example, for data with many-to-many relationship, such as the classical example of students taking courses, relational model offers the most flexible way of presenting such relationship without duplicating data. In a relational model, entity is identified by an id, the ids are recorded in a relationship mapping table to capture many-to-many relationships. With many-to-many relationships, two different hierarchies: the hierarchy of student taking multiple courses and the hierarchy of a course being taken by multiple students can be modeled without data duplication. For OLTP workloads where data is read and updated frequently, relational model with application of high degree of normalization rules is the best model. Therefore, there is no reason to suggest XML model/XQuery as a replacement of the relational model/SQL.

However, the rationale for a DBMS is that it can store and retrieve all kind of data, not just one kind of data. In RDBMS, structure of the data is well-defined so that data and its structure can be separated out cleanly. Structure of data is defined using the relational schema (table definitions) and managed as meta-data by RDBMS. Unstructured content is one extreme of data where there is no meaningful structure to describe the collection of data. Semi-structured data is data whose structure is not easily separable from data because the structure is dynamic and evolving. Semi-structured data is represented by adding tags to mark and annotate the data. The tag denotes inline structures of the data so that they can be referred via navigation of tags. Each tag has a name and tags can form a hierarchy. Querying semi-structured data involve querying tag names, tag hierarchy and data together.

XML data model defines a hierarchical tree composed of nodes having both tag and content. Structure of data is recorded as XML tags annotating the data. Both structure and data can be stored and queried together using XQuery, a declarative language. XML can be used as a canonical data model for representing all: unstructured data, semi-structured data and structured data, in a DWH. The following is a list of key points illustrating how XQuery/XML model differentiates from SQL/Relational model and keyword text search/IR model.

Schema Flexibility: "Data first, schema later or never" approach is the key strength of XML data model that differentiates itself from relational model. Data can be stored and queried without defining schema for the data first. Data annotated with tags become self-describing and self-contained. Data with high schema variability, data with rapidly evolving schema can be modeled using XML model. Schema evolution, which is a common issue for RDBMS administrators and developers, is not an issue for XML model. Although XML can be schema-based, XML schema is primary used for the purpose of data validation instead of being used as relational schema that defines table structures to store XML data. One XML document collection can hold XML document instances without any XML schemas or different XML schemas. This differentiates an XML model from a relational model where one table can hold only entities conforming to one particular relational schema.

Structure Query Capability: In the XML data model, structures are not specified apriori as meta-data. Instead, structures are embedded into the data, therefore, they can be searched and queried as if they were data. Capabilities of wildcard tag name search and descendant tag name search in XQuery essentially support the notation of searching structures without knowing the exact names of the structure or the exact hierarchy of the structure. This differentiates from SQL where exact names of the relational tables that hold the data and exact join column keys to join tables must be specified in the query. Using XQuery on XML, users have the flexibility of writing specific query with precise structural names and hierarchy or generic query without precise structural names and hierarchy. The latter capability gives user the flexibility of querying structures and data together while structure of data is dynamic and evolving.

Full context aware text search Capability: With XQuery full text capability, XML data model is an ideal data model to manage document contents. Classical keyword text search for unstructured content from the IR community lacks declarative language to search content with mark-up tag annotation. However, after document content is modeled as XML document, XQuery full text search can be leveraged to provide hierarchical context-aware full text search with context defined by XML tags. Classical keyword text search capability is logically a degeneration of XQuery full text search over one XML text node capturing the entire unstructured content. Therefore, XQuery/XML model completely subsumes the keyword text search/IR model.

Declarative data transformation and construction: XQuery is an expressive language for not only queries that enable "finding needles in the haystack", but also transformation constructs that enable transformation of existing data, construction of new data in a declarative way. This differentiates from classical keyword text search where there is no declarative language construct to process the searched keywords. Keyword highlighting functionality is not part of the full text language. This also differentiates from SQL where there is no declarative language facilitating hierarchical result construction. Therefore, in the relational model that flattens everything, hierarchical object construction has to be done outside SQL in a procedure-oriented host programming language code. With XML data model and XQuery, hierarchical object construction can be defined declaratively as hierarchical views over the relational model.

In summary, Figure 1 shows the positions and value of XML. Currently unstructured data is stored in LOB column without the need of schema. So they are easy to store, however, there is no strong declarative language, such as SQL, to query them. This falls into NO-SQL approach. Structured data are stored in relational model and is easy to query them using SQL. However, it is relatively hard to store them without coming out schema first. XML sits in the middle to bridge these two worlds and provides value as a flexible data model with declarative XQuery language.

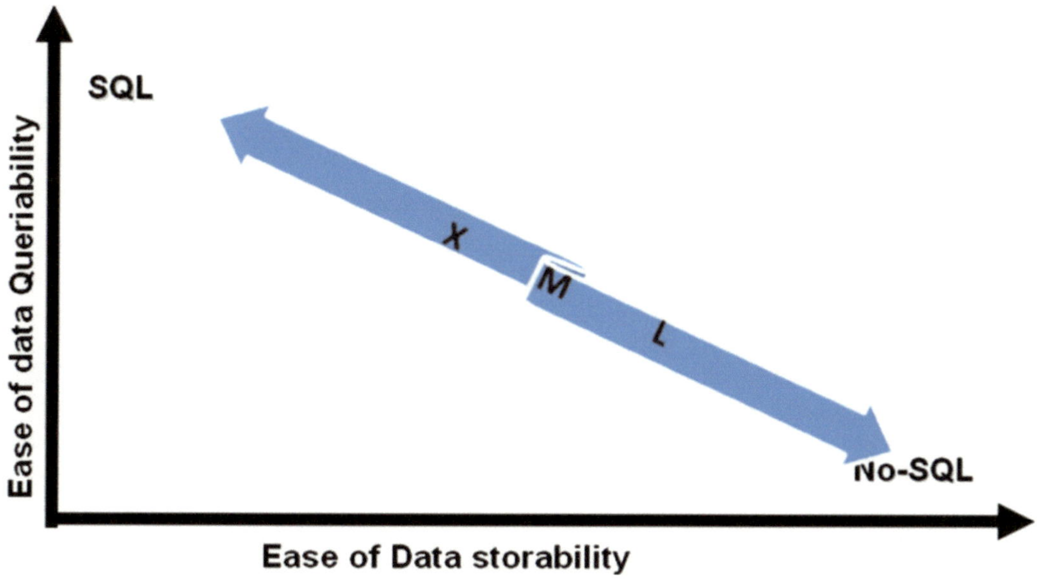

Fig. 1. XML bridges SQL and No-SQL approaches

4.2 Why XML for DWH?

Besides representing semi-structured data and unstructured content, there are advantages to leveraging XML data model to handle DWH processing. We present the key points here.

4.2.1 ETL flexibility

Building DWH requires Extracting, Transforming, and Loading (ETL) of data from multiple data sources. XML is increasingly being used as an exchange format to facilitate data transfer. In the past decade, different industries have defined XML schemas, such as XBRL schema for business reporting, HL7 schema for health industry, FPXML schema for financial industry to capture and exchange domain specific XML data. When an XML schema is rigid, it is possible to shred the XML data into relational tables. However, common industrial XML schema is designed to capture all possible data representations, therefore, industrial XML schema is highly variant with usage of many XML constructs, such as XML nodes of any data type, mixed content data, choice models, etc., so that mapping XML schema into relational schema is either infeasible or will result in the creation of many tables having many null columns that are sparsely populated with data. From the perspective of XML schema, this is reasonable because XML schema is supposed to be used for XML data validation instead of being used to decompose XML into relational data. This indeed highlights the crux of the challenges faced with data integration and extraction. That is, coming up with a small, rigid relational like schema that covers every piece of data variant is not feasible. To overcome this problem, common ETL process for RDBMS DWH store defines a minimal relational schema that captures the most commonly used data. The rest of the data that do not fit the relational schema are either stored in LOB columns or as files in the file system. This results in limited query capability over the non-relational data.

Using an RDBMS that supports XML persistence overcomes the above deficiencies because using XQuery the structure and data in the XML can be queried together. Furthermore, well-structured data in the XML can be extracted into relational tables by building XML indexes on top of XML storage (Liu et al., 2007). **This approach of persisting data as XML first and extracting well-structured data within XML as XMLTable based XMLIndex is the practical means to fulfill the spirit of "data first schema later".**

4.2.2 Integrated structured, semi-structured, unstructured content search query

Query 2 is a SQL query involving both text search and regular relational search. Such a query enables users to integrate well-structured data search based on classical RDBMS technology and unstructured content search query from classical IR technology together. Paper (Yates & Navarro 1996) illustrates the need of integrating contents and structure search tightly in text retrieval. As XQuery full text capability subsumes the classical IR text search capability, Query 3 shows how SQL/XML that provides XQuery capability in SQL is able to do integrated data query regardless of the availability of a pre-defined structure for the data. Description column of the Fact table is of XMLType that stores XML data. The '*. contains text "promotion" ftand "independence"*' is XQuery full text syntax to specify searching the keyword '*promotion*' and '*independence*' anywhere in all the descendent text nodes from the input context node. XMLEXISTS() is a SQL/XML operator that takes as input an XMLType column, which in this case is the Description column of the Fact Table. This predicate executes the XQuery full text functions to see if the evaluation of the text node returns any nodes. If it does, XMLEXISTS() returns the boolean TRUE value.

```
SELECT f.StoreId, count(*)
FROM TransactionFact f, Customers c, Items i, Dates d, Stores s
WHERE f.CustomerId = c.CustomerId AND f.ItemId = i.ItemId AND f.StoreId = s.StoreId AND
f.DateId = d.DateId AND i.ItemName = 'TV' AND s.StoreZipCode >= 45000 and
s.StoreZipCode <= 46000 AND i.ItemPrice < 300 AND d.Year between 2003 and 2005 AND
XMLEXISTS('. contains text "promotion" ftand "independence"' PASSING description)
GROUP BY f.StoreId
```

Query 3. SQL/XML Query on Hybrid XML and Relational Star-Schema

4.2.3 I/O friendly XML object retrieval and object transformation

In a DWH, data is loaded once and read many times. In a typical relational database, to retrieve the original entity data in full, tables are joined over primary keys and foreign keys which results in generation of random I/O requests compared to the option of storing data aggregated and contiguous on disk which results in typically one I/O to bring the whole object entity into memory. Therefore, for a DWH, it is desirable to store data in a de-normalized way compared to an OLTP database where data is normalized to avoid update anomalies. XML persistency essentially extends the idea of de-normalization further by materializing hierarchy without joint keys and thus provides the fastest whole object retrieval from the perspective of disk friendly I/O. *From I/O perspective, excessive seeks with small read per seek is worse in performance compared with few seeks with large read per seek.*

Consider the third phase of processing of Query 1 where the set of RIDs from the Fact table is computed. In addition to fetching the rows from Fact table based on RID, Dimensional table lookup may still be needed to bring in relevant dimensional values using dimension ids stored in the Fact table to re-construct the original transaction object. On the other hand, XML data may be stored in a compressed binary format without shredding the data into relational tables resulting in the advantage of efficient retrieval of the whole object when needed. This form of XML persistency is essentially a generalization of data de-normalization concept in DWH design. Furthermore, XQuery provides constructs to transform XML into different hierarchical shapes and forms for different presentations of the data.

Having discussed the value of XML data model for DWH, we now show the XML and XQuery functionality support in RDBMS leveraging the SQL/XML standard.

4.3 SQL/XML in RDBMS for XML based DWH

SQL/XML is an ISO SQL standard that defines XML as a datatype conforming to the XQuery data model with three new built-in operators: XMLQuery(), XMLExists(), and XMLCast(); and one new table construct - XMLTable to facilitate XQuery invocation in SQL and to query and modify XML datatype. Furthermore, it has introduced new built-in SQL/XML publishing operators: XMLElement(), XMLForest(), XMLComment(), and XMLPI(); and a new built-in aggregation operator - XMLAgg() that facilitate constructing XML from structured relational data. Therefore, with the SQL/XML standard, XML data can be managed by RDBMS along with structured data without the need of a specialized XML database. It is more elegant to enable management of all data in one system, and query them using SQL with domain object extension (such as SQL/XML), than to manage different data in different systems, and to correlate them in the application tier or mid-tier. Indeed, SQL/XML approach reflects the success of object relational approach that provides a type, function, index extensibility framework for managing any data in Object Relational DBMS - ORDBMS (Stonebraker et al., 1998). Contemporary RDBMS supports SQL/XML standard leveraging ORDBMS principle (Krishnaprasad et al., 2005). There are three approaches to supporting SQL/XML in a post-relational DBMS.

4.3.1 Approach 1: Relational and XML hybrid

In this approach, the relational table is extended with XMLType column instead of LOB column to store content that do not have rigid schema to be shredded into relational columns. This approach is conservative and represents the first generational adoption of XML in RDBMS. Query 3 shows this approach. It has the advantage of specifying both SQL and XQuery declaratively in one query. However, like processing of Query 2, processing

Query 3 still requires the two-part processing strategies, that is, join of relational indexing for relational part of the query and XML indexing for XML part of the query. Furthermore, the conceptual issue with this hybrid approach is that in many cases, structured data and unstructured data are embedded within each other, i.e. there could be islands of structured data embedded in top-level unstructured content. Therefore, it is natural to store the whole top-level data as one XML object and only project out the islands of structured data as index. This leads to Approach2 discussed below.

4.3.2 Approach 2: XML persistence with XML table based XMLIndex

Approach1 reveals the underlying problem that structures inside XML can be too diverse to be captured by relational tables. In this approach, the XML is stored as is, while an XML Index is created to index the islands of structured data for relational processing. XQuery can be used to declaratively specify the extraction of the structured data from the XML in the XML Index creation.

For example, consider that the purchase transaction captured in table 1,2,3,4,5 is stored as one XML document, shown in XML-Document 1 below, in a table containing all XML documents.

```
<Transaction>
<Customer id = 1454>
        <CustomerName>John Smith</CustomerName>
</Customer>
<Store storied =123>
        <StoreName>Electronic-Supply</StoreName>
        <StoreZipCode>45789</StoreZipCode>
</Store>
 <Item ItemId=1456>
        <ItemName>T.V</ItemName>
         <ItemPrice>250.32</ItemPrice>
         <QuantitySold>2</QuantitySold>
 </Item>
<poDate dateId=13579>2004-07-20</poDate>
 <sale_comment>
This is sold via special summer sale promotion program at the store. The promotion program is conducted along with the independence celebration event in the city.
</sale_comment>
</Transaction>
```

XML-Document 1. Transaction Fact

We create a transactions table having an XMLType column that stores each transaction fact as an XML document in a row. Then we create XMLTable based XMLIndex to extract structured data out into a relational table: TransactionFact as shown in SQL-DDL 1. The XML Index uses XMLTable construct with XPath/XQuery. The equivalent of Query 3 is now formulated as Query 4 using the XMLTable construct. In Query 4, the original fact table in Query 3 becomes a virtual table computed by XMLTable() construct over XMLType column.

```
Create table Transactions(xmldata XMLType);

Create Index tabIdx on Transactions(xmldata) as
(transactionfact XMLTable('/Transaction'
                  column
                     CustomerId varchar(20) PATH 'Customer/@id',
                     ItemId varchar(20)  PATH 'Item/@ItemId',
                     StoreId varchar(20)  PATH 'Store/@storeid',
                     DateId  integer PATH 'poDate/@dateId',
                     QuantitySold integer PATH 'Item/QuantitySold')
);
```

SQL-DDL 1. XMLTable based XMLIndex Creation

```
SELECT f.StoreId, count(*)
FROM Transactions,
XMLTable('/Transaction' PASSING Transactions.xmldata
      Column
        CustomerId varchar(20) 'PATH Customer/@id',
        ItemId varchar(20) PATH 'Item/@ItemId',
        StoreId varchar(20) PATH 'Store/@storeid',
         DateId  integer PATH 'poDate/@dateId',
         QuantitySold integer PATH 'Item/QuantitySold') Fact f,
Customers c, Items i, Dates d, Stores s
WHERE f.CustomerId = c.CustomerId AND f.ItemId = i.ItemId AND f.StoreId = s.StoreId AND
f.DateId = d.DateId AND i.ItemName = 'TV' AND s.StoreZipCode >= 45000 and
s.StoreZipCode <= 46000 AND i.ItemPrice < 300 AND d.Year between 2003 and 2005 AND
XMLEXISTS('. contains text "promotion" ftand "independence"' PASSING description)
GROUP BY f.StoreId
```

Query 4. SQL/XML Query on XML Persistency with XMLTable

Compared to the hybrid approach, this XML persistency approach with XMLTable based XMLIndex has the following advantages for DWH environment:

- There is no need to force all data into a common integration schema; all data can be captured without any data loss.
- XMLTable based XML index can be used to index the islands of structured data. This results in a flexible mechanism because index can be dropped and re-created without affecting the base storage. Users have the flexibility to decide what to index and how to index without the need for changing the base XML persistency. This genuinely fulfills the goal of 'data first, schema later' approach. Such an approach is superior to that of a relational approach because data can be stored without first defining the schema. Yet, it does not lose the advantage of relational processing because the projection of the embedded structured data as an index allows for queries over this data to be processed using relational access methods. (Liu et al., 2006). XMLTable based XMLIndex conceptually represents partial relational shredding approach of XML. Furthermore, it gives users the flexibility of not decomposing XML relationally even if XML is well-structured.

- For a DWH, where data is not frequently modified, maintenance of the XMLTable based XMLIndex is acceptable. For cases where the index definition is complex enough requiring more time to be processed, XMLIndex can be maintained like materialized views that can be refreshed asynchronously.
- Finally, all existing business intelligence tools on current relational model based DWH are completely useable on XML via the XMLTable constructs supported by XMLTable based XMLIndex.

4.3.3 Approach 3: XML persistence with XML-extended Inverted Index (XEIIX)

This approach uses the same XML persistence as that of Approach 2. Approach 2 above still conceptually requires users to split structured query from full text query, and therefore forces users to write the query to explicitly join the two parts of the query together. In Approach 3, using XQuery on XML, it is feasible to express the structures and unstructured data query intermixed naturally and natively as shown in Query 5.

```
SELECT XMLCAST(XMLQUERY('$doc/Transaction/StoreId') AS INTEGER) as StoreId,
count(*)
FROM Transactions
WHERE XMLExists('$doc/Transaction[Item/ItemName = "TV" and fn:year-from-
dateTime(poDate) >= 2003 and fn:year-from-dateTime(poDate) <= 2005 and
xs:integer(StoreZipCode) >=45000 and xs:integer(StoreZipCode) <= 46000 and
saleComment contains text "promotion" ftand "independence" ]'
            PASSING description AS "doc")
GROUP BY StoreId
```

Query 5. SQL/XML Query on XML Persistency with Full XQuery

The significance of Query 5 is that there is no explicit relational join query specified in SQL FROM clause. From the perspective of user, it is more natural to express structured and unstructured data query using Query 5 instead of Query 4. This illustrates the advantages of XML as a hierarchical data model and XQuery as a user friendly language to access hierarchical structures using XPath syntax instead of specifying explicit joins of relational tables. Internally RDBMS can either process XPath relationally by decomposing XPath traversal as joins of relational tables, if XML is indexed relationally, or by processing XPath natively if XML is persisted in aggregated binary form. Although XQuery and SQL/XML processing can be decomposed into storage/index independent query logical rewrite transformation followed by storage/index dependent physical rewrite transformation (Liu et.al, 2008), from the user's perspective, the query is written independent of physical storage/index methods. To process Query 5 efficiently, however, we need to extend inverted text index to support XML; such an XML extended inverted index (XEIIX) is discussed in section 5.

5. Efficient processing of DWH query on structured and unstructured data

In this section, we discuss the extended inverted (XEIIX) index layout to efficiently process both structured and unstructured data search. XEIIX is an extension of the classical inverted text index to index structured data, XML hierarchies and keywords in unstructured content all together.

5.1 Comparison of bitmap join index, columnar storage and IR inverted text index

Before we go into XML Extended Inverted Index (XEIIX), let's look at the following three common query processing strategies in RDBMS and IR systems to motivate the rationale for developing XEIIX.

Bitmap Join Index: Recall that in the bitmap join index approach presented in section 3.1.3, to efficiently process star-join in DWH, each row in the Fact table is mapped to a ROP (Row Ordinal Position). Each bitmap index maps a set of dimension values of a given dimension to ROPs. SQL *and, or, not* boolean predicates for different dimension values are processed using set-based multi-dimensional joins. The set-based multi-dimensional join is done efficiently by computing intersection, union and difference among a set of bitmaps. Bitmap join-index representation is very compact and thus requires less amount of disk I/O.

Columnar Storage: Columnar storage (Stonebraker et al., 2005) for DWH is a similar approach that uses invisible join strategy to process star-schema join query (Abadi et al., 2008). All values of a column of the base table are stored together in a compressed form to reduce the amount of disk I/Os to read them into memory. Each column value is implicitly identified by its corresponding ROP of the row containing that column value. Fast scan of columnar data using small amount of disk I/O results in a set of bitmaps representing ROPs for rows that match the given dimension ids. The multi-dimension join is then done efficiently using bitmap intersections.

IR Inverted text index: Each document stored in the base table row is given a document id (DOCID). The DOCID is identical to the ROP, It is a unique sequential integer identifying each document using the position of the row that contains the document. Inverted text index maps a keyword to a posting-list which consists of a set of sorted DOCIDs that identify documents that contain the keyword (Zobel & Moffat, 2006). The posting-list is delta-compressed leveraging the sequential integer property of the DOCID. This results in small amount of disk I/Os. Keyword search query using '*and, or, not*' predicate is done via pre-sorted merge join among posting-lists (Zobel & Moffat, 2006).

All three presented techniques have the following common query processing and indexing properties:

- They all handle boolean predicates of *and, or, not* on a set of dimension values extracted from a collection of objects. In RDBMS, each table can be considered as a collection and each row of the table can be considered as an object. The dimension values are column values extracted from each row. In an IR system, each document collection can be considered as a collection, and each document can be considered as an object. The dimension values are keywords extracted from each document.
- They identify each collection object using a unique sequential integer, henceforth referred to as DOCID. There exists an I/O friendly layout of a mapping structure so that looking up the mapping between a dimension value to a set of DOCIDs having the dimension value is very efficient. In RDBMS, the mapping structure is either bitmap join index or columnar layout of relational table. The mapping structure in IR system is an inverted text index. Although the mapping structure can be logically modeled as a relational table, storing each mapping as a row in the relational table causes poor performance due to the on-disk layout of the table rows. This is one of the key reasons

why an IR text index layout using a relational table could be an order of magnitude slower than a customized text search engine implementation (Brewer 2005). In fact, contemporary RDBMS products that support inverted text index do not store keyword and DOCID mapping as individual rows in a relational table. Instead, the disk layout of posting list of the inverted text index is highly compressed and stored in LOB structures. Therefore, it requires small amount of disk I/O to fetch the entire posting list into memory.

- They all process boolean *and, or, not* predicates on dimension values using set intersection, union and difference computation among sets of DOCIDs or bitmaps identified by ROPs. This set join processing essentially converts the polynomial-bound multiple binary-joins into a linear bound multi-way join. The inverted text index's posting list for a given keyword stores DOCIDs in a sorted order. The bitmap positions stored in bitmap join index for a given dimension value stores ROPs in sorted order. Therefore, DOCIDs are pre-sorted in all of these approaches and the linear multi-way join is an effectively pre-sorted merge join (Sort-merge join has linear join property excluding the sorting time.). Paper (Zhang et al., 2001) shows that Multi-Predicate Merge Join strategy commonly employed by full text search engine with hardware cache utilization are the two key reasons that conventional relational engines with conventional join methods do not yield comparable performance to a full text search engine. Furthermore, hardware based vector instructions can be leveraged to further accelerate multi-way join process. For example, bitmap join, can be speedup by using hard-ware vector processing instructions.

It has also been shown that inverted index is more space efficient and delivers better query performance than that of bitmap index when the attribute indexed has a high cardinality (Bjørklund et al., 2009). This leads to the conclusion that applying IR inverted index to DWH is a fruitful direction to take.

5.2 XML-extended inverted index (XEIIX)

Having examined the above three cases, we propose to process the structured and unstructured DWH query 5 in a disk I/O friendly manner based on Multi-Predicate Pre-Sorted Merge join (MPPSMJ), a technique, employed by customized inverted index text engines.

We extend the classical inverted text index to form the XEIIX. The XML element and attribute tags are indexed as regular keywords. All XML text content is indexed by their keywords. There is already keyword position stored in posting list in classical inverted text index so that phrase search is done by comparing keyword position information during MPPSMJ process (Zobel & Moffat, 2006). The XEIIX contains XML tag hierarchical position information so that keyword and XPath containment is processed during MPPSMJ process. Parent-child relationship between XML tags can also be tracked in the index so as to speed up hierarchical relationship check. The key idea behind XEIIX is that it captures both XML structures (tags and their hierarchical relationships) and content data together in one index. With such an integrated index, the search of structure and data together can be processed efficiently, thereby realizing the full potential of XML and XQuery. From a RDBMS perspective, being able to query without differentiating structures and data is a conceptual milestone. From an IR perspective, being able to do content search within structures so that text search becomes context aware is also a conceptual milestone.

But there is still one thing missing in that classical full text search is not capable of performing range predicates using common scalar datatypes, such as, number, date, time, etc, that are widely used in RDBMS. However, XQuery supports the capability of querying data embedded in XML using datatype aware range predicate. For example, to process XQuery expressions of Query 5, such as *'fn:year-from-dateTime(poDate) >= 2003 and fn:year-from-dateTime(poDate) <= 2005 and xs:integer(StoreZipCode) >=45000 and xs:integer(StoreZipCode) <= 46000'*, we need to further enhance the XEIIX to index range type data embedded in XML. Even for XQuery expression *'Item/ItemName = "TV"'*, *ItemName* range comparison is performed using character string datatype which is semantically different from full text search because full text search is subject to stemming, thesaurus, diacritics, etc. options supported by a text search engine.

We, therefore, propose to enhance XEIIX to also index well-defined relational data in the XML document. The XMLTable construct used in XMLTable based XMLIndex presented in section 4.3.2 can be used as a conceptual framework to allow users to declaratively locate the data to be indexed as range-typed data. This is shown in SQL-DDL2 as an illustrative syntax to create XEIIX covering relational scalar datatypes data. However, unlike XMLTable based XMLIndex that physically implements the index as relational tables, the index layout is exactly the same as that of mapping a keyword to a posting list of sorted DOCIDs. The range-data index structure maps a range typed data value to a set of sorted DOCIDs having that value. The MPPSMJ processing can join posting lists for both ranged-typed data and text keywords. This essentially accomplishes the integration of structured data query and unstructured content search at the index level. This integrated index approach performs better than the conventional approach of evaluating structured predicates using relational indexes and retrieving ROWIDS and evaluating text predicates using Text indexes and retrieving DOCIDs and then finally joining DOCIDs and ROWIDs. The XEIIX structure and the MPPSMJ process essentially flattens all joins uniformly using DOCIDs. In fact, both the bitmap index join approach and invisible join in columnar storage for pure relational queries have demonstrated the performance advantage of doing join using ROPs instead of ROWIDs due to small sequential I/O traffic and linear-bound MPPSMJ join. From this perspective, XEIIX leverages the benefits of both the bitmap join-index in RDBMS and inverted text inedex in IR. This is an efficient design to fulfill the goal of XQuery with full text capability that tightly integrates both structured data query and unstructured content search together that otherwise would have to been done separately (one in RDBMS and one in IR) and joined in the end.

```
Create Index xml-text-index on Transactions(xmldata) as
(xmlfull text,
Range-data: XMLTable('/Transaction'
                column
                   ItemName varchar(20) PATH 'Item/ItemName',
                   StoreZipCode integer PATH 'Store/StoreZipCode',
                   Year integer PATH 'fn:year-from-dateTime(poDate/@dateId)'
                   )
);
```

SQL-DDL 2. XML-extended Inverted Index

5.3 Declarative & efficient object construction and transformation

Because the relational model normalizes entity objects into a set of tables, in an RDBMS, in order to re-create the original entity object, one has to issue a SQL query that joins the tables and selects all the columns out into the mid-tier where a host programming language is used to construct the original object entity. In a DWH star-join query, the retrieval of the original transactional object entails pulling columns of both the fact transaction table and all the dimensional tables. This is illustrated in the SQL example in Query 6. If all fields of an entity object needs to be retrieved in the end, one of the challenges for an RDBMS using columnar storage is to develop efficient materialization strategies to delay the row construction (Abadi et al., 2007).

```
SELECT c.CustomerId, c.CustomerName, d.Date, d.Month, d.Year, s.StoreZipCode, f.Description
FROM TransactionFact f, Customers c, Items i, Dates d, Stores s
WHERE f.CustomerId = c.CustomerId AND f.ItemId = i.ItemId AND f.StoreId = s.StoreId AND
f.DateId = d.DateId AND i.ItemName = 'TV' AND s.StoreZipCode >= 45000 and
s.StoreZipCode <= 46000 AND i.ItemPrice < 300 AND d.Year between 2003 and 2005 AND
CONTAINS(description, 'promotion')
```

Query 6. SQL All Fields Selection

To contrast, now consider the SQL/XML queries, supported by an XRDBMS, illustrated below in Query 7 and Query 8. Query 7 shows the usage of XQuery in the select list to selectively project out fields from the original stored XML to construct new XML objects. Query 8 illustrates the capability in XQuery to transform the original XML object into a new object by deleting the *sale_comment* node.

In comparison to Query 6, Query 7 and 8 illustrate the following advantages of an XRDBMS and XQuery over RDBMS and SQL:

- The XML support in XRDBMS frees the user from figuring out exactly what tables to join which depends on how the transaction object has been normalized into relational tables. XML preserves the abstraction of the entity object, and enables the user to issue a query based on this abstraction using XQuery, which is then efficiently processed by the XRDBMS using XEIIX l and MPPSMJ process.
- XRDBMS allows users to construct new object or transform objects declaratively using XQuery instead of programmatically constructing or transforming the object in the mid-tier by issuing a relational SQL query in a plain RDBMS, The I/O efficiency in an XRDBMS is realized by storing XML in a compressed binary form that can be loaded into memory using a smaller amount of I/O. Then all XQuery evaluation in the select list is performed on the in-memory XML object. This is in contrast to the columnar storage of an RDBMS where various pieces of the column values need to be fetched from disk and assembled in the end. In this regard, it may be argued that it is a better option for the RDBMS to use columnar store as an index rather than as a persistence mechanism, thereby taking advantage of the columnar layout of data for efficient evaluation of predicates while avoiding the overhead of piecing the columns together by going to the row storage for retrieving the entire row. **Therefore, we think columnar index instead of columnar storage is the ideal way to bridge row store and column store.** In this way, not only row filtering that leverages the disk I/O friendly columnar layout of columns and invisible bitmap joins can be done efficiently, but also full row retrieval can be done efficiently without unnecessary assembly from columnar storage as well!

```
SELECT XMLQUERY(
'<TVTransaction>
(
<Customer @id = {$doc/Transaction/Customer/@id}>
    <CName>{$doc/Customer/CustomerName/text()}</CName>
</Customer>
,
<transactionDate>{$doc/Transaction/poDate/text()}</transactionDate>
<zip>{$doc/Transaction/Store/StoreZipCode/text()}</zip>
,
$doc/<sale_comment>
)
</TVTransaction>'
PASSING description AS "doc")
FROM Transactions
WHERE XMLExists('$doc/Transaction[Item/ItemName = "TV" and fn:year-from-dateTime(poDate) >= 2003 and fn:year-from-dateTime(poDate) <= 2005 and xs:integer(StoreZipCode) >=45000 and xs:integer(StoreZipCode) <= 46000 and saleComment contains text "promotion" ftand "independence" ]' PASSING description AS "doc")
```

Query 7. SQL/XML Query with XML Construction

```
SELECT XMLQUERY(
'copy $cpy := $doc modify
      delete nodes $cpy/sale_comment
 return $cpy'
PASSING description AS "doc")
FROM Transactions
WHERE XMLExists('$doc/Transaction[Item/ItemName = "TV" and fn:year-from-dateTime(poDate) >= 2003 and fn:year-from-dateTime(poDate) <= 2005 and xs:integer(StoreZipCode) >=45000 and xs:integer(StoreZipCode) <= 46000 and saleComment contains text "promotion" ftand "independence" ]' PASSING description AS "doc")
```

Query 8. SQL/XML Query with XML Transformation

6. Challenges and future directions

In this section, we discuss the challenges and future work for Data Warehousing and business intelligence.

6.1 Domain specific object type handling

So far, we have discussed the rationale for extending DWH technology to cover both structured and unstructured data,with integrated search over both data. However, we focused on only data of scalar and text data types. There are domain specific data, such as spatial, image, etc. that can be embedded inside XML documents. There is valuable information stored in these domain specific objects that need to be semantically queried and analyzed together with scalar and text data to assist making intelligent business decisions. ORDBMS (Stonebraker et al., 1998) framework enables the addition of user defined types to model domain specific objects, user defined functions on user defined types to manipulate such objects, and user defined index (domain index) with user defined operators to speed up queries over such objects. The end result is that ORDBMS appears to understand domain specific object types as if they were native built-in types with built-in functions, operators and indices. For example, an ORDBMS may be extended to support management of Multi-media data, images, and handle queries over such data with matching and resemblance operators that are efficiently evaluated using domain indexes created over such data (Candan & Sapino 2010). Modern ORDBMS also manage spatial objects that are built on the domain index and extensibility framework (Kanth et al., 1999, Kanth et al., 2002). The one point to highlight is that the domain index probes in a typical ORDBMS return ROWIDs that are then used to map and merge with the rest of the SQL query evaluation and execution.

Built on the same principle of ORDBMS and Object Relational SQL, XRDBMS and XQuery have built-in extensibility to support user defined type and user defined functions. This enables queries over structured, unstructured and domain specific object instances all together using XQuery and SQL/XML. However, the key difference is that in an XRDBMS, the XEIIX returns a set of DOCIDs instead of ROWIDs. Whereas the domain index described return a set of ROWIDs. One way to handle this is to convert DOCIDs into ROWIDs and then join them together. However, ROWID joins are slower than DOCIDs and also incur the cost of conversions between DOCIDs and ROWIDs. Pre-sorted merge join techniques on sorted DOCID is much faster than general purpose ROWID joins. Future work is needed to investigate the best way of joining domain specific index results with inverted text index results, that is, whether MPPSMJ can be extended to cover domain indices. An even more fundamental question is whether the inverted style index that we described handling both text content and structured data can be extended to cover domain specific indexing as well.

6.2 XML in text mining, enterprise document search and information extraction

Enterprise search crawls document data from various data sources, builds inverted text index to facilitate keyword search based on classical I/R techniques (Salton & McGill, 1983). Structured data within the documents, such as document authors, types, publishing dates etc, are extracted out to provide facet navigational search. Text mining does statistical analysis of document content to derive concepts and topics contained in the document collection. Entity and relationship extraction from documents provide foundation for text mining and pattern discovery. All of the derivative data from these unstructured content analysis and discovery process need to be captured and persisted so that they could be queried and analyzed. These derivative data can be retained in context of the document they were discovered in via XML. Future work is needed to investigate how XML can be effectively used as a data model to facilitate text mining and analytical work.

6.3 Real-time DWH support

So far we have seen that DWH assumes read-only batch update model where decisions are made based on relatively stale data. The challenge is to support near real-time DWH given that all index and data layout in DWH do not favor in-place updates of the data. We think that the timestamp based consistent read query semantics and in-memory indexing with batch index merges is the direction worth exploring.

First, data is not in place updated. Instead updating data implies a new version of the data is inserted and old version of the data is marked for deletion. Queries run with an implicit timestamp so that the query results are consistent, although it may not always correspond to the latest timestamp. With timestamp based data version technique, the database would essentially allow time traversal query where history could be queried. Consistent read is well-practiced in RDBMS (Bamford 1992), so is time traversal query capability (Gawlick 2004).

Second, index for new version of data is built in memory and periodically merged with on-disk index structures. Such incremental index maintenance is discussed in inverted text index implementations (Zobel & Moffat 2006). The challenge is how such technique can be applied to other domain specific indexing structures. We believe that for DWH environment, data may never fit in memory, but index in compressed form can fit in memory resulting in fast query and search.

7. Generic star schema and star query

Classical DWH practices develop schema first and then load data later. In this chapter, we have shown we can do data store first via XML persistency and exploit schema later via different XML indexing methods. The XML Index can be a relational projection of XML to facilitate relational modeling over XML - this is the idea of the XMLTable based XMLIndex discussed in section 4.3.2. The XML Index can be keyword and tag extractions to facilitate context aware text search over XML - this is the idea of XML extended inverted text index discussed in section 5.2. The XML Index can also project out domain specific object instances embedded in XML to facilitate domain object specific query as discussed in section 6.1. Therefore, generalizing all this, we think the future DWH practice is going to be a more ***generic star-schema*** where the fact table is a collection of XML documents, each of which is identified by a DOCID. Different dimensional tables represent different dimension values extracted from the base XML document, and thus a dimensional table serves as the role of a ***dimension index*** into the XML document collection. The dimension value can be as simple as well-typed relational data or can be as complex as domain specific data. Text keywords and XML tags are default dimensional index. The dimensional index maps a dimensional value to a set of pre-sorted DOCIDs that satisfy a relationship with the dimensional values. That relationship is essentially an operator that can be evaluated via the dimensional index. The ***generic star-query*** is on the single fact table with where clauses of a set of boolean predicates, each of which specifies a domain index specific operator searching on some dimension values. The generic star-query is first processed via probing different dimensional indexes, followed by computing the set of common DOCIDs using pre-sorted merge joins among sets of pre-sorted DOCIDs obtained from dimension index lookup. The DOCIDs are then used to retrieve base XML document upon which further data extraction, transformation and aggregation operations in the query select list are performed. All of these phases of processing can be executed in parallel, and may exploit specific hardware accelerations when feasible. New dimensional index can be added as new dimensions are discovered for the underlying data. Dimensional index can be dropped when such dimension search is not needed. Thus this generic star-schema/query model fully embraces the concept of data first, schema later.

8. Conclusion

In this chapter, we have shown that XML is flexible enough to handle both structured and unstructured data. Declarative XQuery language with SQL/XML can be used to effectively build and query data warehouses comprising of all enterprise data. Both structured data and unstructured content can be managed by one XRDBMS - an XML enabled RDBMS with XQuery and SQL/XML. This obviates the need to migrate relational data into a pure XML database; instead an XML view over relational data can be defined. Unstructured and semi-structured data can be stored natively as XML, without relational shredding, in the XRDBMS. All XML data can be uniformly queried via XQuery using SQL/XML. XML extended inverted text index can be used to efficiently support XQuery processing. SQL/XML bridges the structured and unstructured world: relational data can be viewed as XML via SQL/XML view, and XML data can be cast as relational data via XMLTable construct. This provides for a very flexible system that enables all relational tools and application to access XML Data while new XML tools and applications can access both XML and relational data.

Various industries are defining XML Schemas for data exchange, transformation and reporting. Domain specific object instances can be embedded in XML. Such XML data can be persisted as native XML in XRDBMS and then queried using XQuery, or relationally using SQL/XML via the XMLTable construct. The management of XML in an extended Relational Database Management system is benefitted by the leverage of secular DBMS technologies, such as data partitioning, parallel query execution, clustered server operating environments, etc. all of which are generally available in a contemporary RDBMS.

To efficiently support DWH query over any data, the design has to realize the significant performance gap between disk I/O and CPU speed. Therefore, I/O friendly data and index layout and pre-sorted multi-way merge join processing remain to be the two key strategies to deliver superior query performance over large volume of data. This really leads to the confluence of inverted text index and its query processing strategies from SIGIR community and columnar oriented data/index layout and its query processing strategies from DBMS SIGMOD community. The integration of the two shall deliver high performance of query that spans structured data and context aware full text search together.

XML and XQuery efforts have led us to explore a new post-relational world where business intelligence over structured, semi-structured and unstructured data is becoming feasible. This post-relational world requires us to embrace the concept of data first, schema later model and to provide declarative query that integrates structure and content search, transformation together. This genuine spirit from post-relational world shall empower business to access and make decisions over any type of data in a unified way.

9. References

Abadi, D.J.; Madden, S; Hachem, N : Column-stores vs. row-stores: how different are they really? SIGMOD Conference 2008: 967-980

Abadi, D.J; Myers, D.S; , DeWitt, D.J.; Madden, S: Materialization Strategies in a Column-Oriented DBMS. ICDE 2007: 466-475

Bamford, R: Using Multiversioning to Improve Performance Without Loss of Consistency. SIGMOD Conference 1992: 164

Bjørklund, T.A; Grimsmo, N; Gehrke, J; Torbjørnsen, Ø: Inverted indexes vs. bitmap indexes in decision support systems. CIKM 2009: 1509-1512

Brewer E.: *Combining Systems and Databases: A Search Engine Retrospective In readings in Database Systems.* The MIT Press, 4th edition, 2005.

Candan, K. S; Sapino, M.L: Data Management for Multimedia Retrieval, Cambridge University Press, ISBN-10: 0521887399, ISBN-13: 978-0521887397 May 31, 2010

Chen P.: *The Enity-Relationship Model: Toward a Unified View of Data.* VLDB 1975: 173

Codd, E. *A Relational Model of Data for Large Shared Data Banks.* Commun. ACM 13(6): 377-387 (1970)

DeWitt, D.J; Gray, J: Parallel Database Systems: *The Future of High Performance Database Systems.* Commun. ACM 35(6): 85-98 (1992)

Gawlick, D: Querying the Past, the Present, and the Future. ICDE 2004: 867

Kanth, K.V.R; Ravada, S; Abugov, D: Quadtree and R-tree indexes in oracle spatial: a comparison using GIS data. SIGMOD Conference 2002: 546-557

Kanth, K.V.R; Ravada, S; Sharma, J; Banerjee, J: Indexing Medium-dimensionality Data in Oracle. SIGMOD Conference 1999: 521-522

Krishnaprasad, M; Liu, Z.H; Manikutty, A; Warner, J.W; Arora, V: *Towards an Industrial Strength SQL/XML Infrastructure.* ICDE 2005: 991-1000

Liu, Z.H; Chandrasekar, S; Baby, T; Chang, H.J: Towards a physical XML independent XQuery/SQL/XML engine. PVLDB 1(2): 1356-1367 (2008)

Liu, Z. H; Krishnaprasad, M; Chang, H.J.; Arora, V: *XMLTable Index An Efficient Way of Indexing and Querying XML Property Data.* ICDE 2007: 1194-1203

Milenova, B.L; Yarmus, J; Campos, Marcos: *SVM In Oracle Database 10g: Removing the Barriers to Widespread Adoption of Support Vector Machines.* VLDB 2005; 1152-1163

Myers, D: (1986) *Psychology,* Worth Publishers, Inc, ISBN: 0-87901-311-7, New York, New York 10003

O'Neil, P.; Graefe, G. *Multi-Table Joins Through Bitmapped Join Indices.* SIGMOD Record, Vol. 24, No.3, Sep 1995

Salton, G; McGill, M: (1983) *Introduction To Modern Information Retrieval,* McGraw-Hill, Inc. ISBN: 0-07-054484-0, U.S.A

SQL/XML: I.O. for Standardization (ISO). Information Technology-Database Language SQL-Part 14: XML-Related Specifications

Seshadri, P; Hellerstein, J.M; Pirahesh, H; Leung, T.Y, C; , Ramakrishnan, R; Srivastava, D; Stuckey, P; Sudarshan, S: *Cost-Based Optimization for Magic: Algebra and Implementation.* SIGMOD Conference 1996: 435-446

Stonebraker, M., Abadi, D, Batkin, A., Chen, X., Cherniack, M, Ferreira, M., Lau, E., Lin, A., Madden, S; O'Neil, E.; O'Neil, P.; Rasin, A.; Tran, N.; Zdonik, S. *C-Store: A Column-oriented DBMS.* VLDB 2005: 553-564

Stonebraker, M; , Brown, P; Moore, D. *Object-Relational DBMSs,* Second Edition Morgan Kaufmann 1998

Stonebraker, M.; Hellerstein, J. *What Goes Around Comes Around.* In readings in Database Systems. The MIT Press, 4th edition, 2005.

XQuery. http://www.w3.org/TR/xquery/

XQuery and XPath Full Text. http://www.w3.org/TR/xpath-full-text-10/

Yates, R.; Navarro, G. *Integrating Contents and Structure in Text Retrieval.* SIGMOD Record, Vol.25, No.1, Mar 1996

Zhang, C.; Naughton, J; DwWitt, D; Luo, Qiong; Lohman, G. *On Supporting Containment Queries in Relational Database Management Systems*. SIGMOD Conference 2001: 425-436

Zobel, J; Moffat, A. *Inverted files for text search engines*. ACM Comput. Surv. 38(2): (2006)

5

Density-Based Clustering and Anomaly Detection

Lian Duan
University of Iowa,
USA

1. Introduction

As of 1996, when a special issue on density-based clustering was published (DBSCAN) (Ester et al., 1996), existing clustering techniques focused on two categories: partitioning methods, and hierarchical methods. Partitioning clustering attempts to break a data set into K clusters such that the partition optimizes a given criterion. Besides difficulty in choosing the proper parameter K, and incapacity of discovering clusters with arbitrary shape, partitioning clustering techniques are very sensitive to outliers. Although the k-medoids method (Kaufman & Rousseeuw, 1990) is more robust than k-means (MacQueen, 1967) in the presence of outliers, they cannot discover outliers. Hierarchical clustering algorithms produce a nested sequence of clusters, with a single all-inclusive cluster at the top and single point clusters at the bottom. CURE (Guha et al., 1998) is capable of finding clusters of arbitrary shapes and reduces the effect of outliers; however, it only considers cluster proximity yet ignores cluster interconnectivity, and an outlier is still assigned to the cluster which has the closest representative point to it.

To discover clusters with arbitrary shape and outliers, density-based clustering methods have been developed. These typically regard clusters as dense regions of objects in the data space that are separated by regions of low density (representing outliers or noises). DBSCAN grows clusters according to a density-based connectivity analysis. OPTICS (Ankerst et al., 1999) extends DBSCAN to produce a cluster ordering obtained from a wide range of parameter settings. DENCLUE (Hinneburg & Keim, 1998) clusters objects based on a set of density distribution functions. LOF (Breunig et al., 2000) uses a more meaningful way to assign to each object a degree of being an outlier than to consider being an outlier as a binary property. LDBSCAN (Duan et al., 2007) combines the concepts of DBSCAN and LOF to discover clusters and outliers. There are two potential benefits of combining clustering and outlier detection: increasing precision and facilitating data understanding. The goal of this chapter is to survey the core concepts and techniques in the density-based clustering and outlier detection (Duan et al., 2009) with its roots in data mining, statistics, machine learning and other communities.

This chapter is organized as follows. Section 2 presents the algorithm LDBSCAN. Section 3 discusses the cluster-based outlier detection. The comprehensive experiments on the algorithms we proposed are conducted on both synthetic data and practical data. Finally, we present some concluding remarks.

2. LDBSCAN: Local-Density-Based Spatial Clustering of Applications with Noise

In this section, we introduce our algorithm LDBSCAN. First, the basic notions used in LDBSCAN are discuss. Then, the algorithm is presented.

2.1 Basic notions of LDBSCAN

2.1.1 Problems of existing density-based algorithms

A common property of many practical data sets is that their intrinsic cluster structures cannot be characterized by global density parameters. As a result, very different local densities may be needed to reveal clusters in different regions of the data space. For example, in the data set depicted in Figure 1, it is impossible to detect the cluster A, B, C_1, C_2, and C_3 simultaneously by using one global density parameter. A global density-based decomposition can only detect the clusters A, B, and C, or C_1, C_2, and C_3. For the second partition, the objects from A and B are noise.

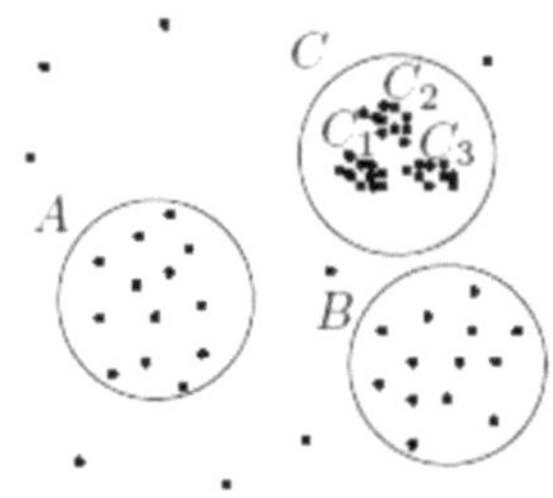

Fig. 1. Clusters with respect to different global density parameters

Optics can solve this problem; however, it only creates an augmented ordering of the database representing its density-based clustering structure instead of producing clusters of a data set explicitly. In addition, it might not be able to generate the clusters resided in other clusters appropriately and this part will be discussed in the experimental part. Therefore, an algorithm which can detect A, B, C_1, C_2, and C_3 explicitly is needed.

2.1.2 Definition of LRD and LOF

The LOF of each object represents the degree the object is being outlying and the LRD of each object represents the local-density of the object. The formal definitions for these notions of LOF and LRD are shortly introduced in the following. More details are provided in (Breunig et al., 2000).

Definition 1 (*k*-distance of an object *p*) For any positive integer *k*, the *k*-distance of object *p*, denoted as *k-distance(p)*, is defined as the distance $d(p,o)$ between *p* and an object $o \in D$ such that:

1. for at least *k* objects $o' \in D \setminus \{p\}$ it holds that $d(p,o') \leq d(p,o)$
2. for at most *k-1* objects $o' \in D \setminus \{p\}$ it holds that $d(p,o') < d(p,o)$.

Definition 2 (*k*-distance neighborhood of an object *p*): Given the *k*-distance of *p*, the *k*-distance neighborhood of *p* contains every object whose distance from *p* is not greater than the k-distance, i.e. $N_{k\text{-}distance(p)}(p)=\{ q \in D \setminus \{p\} \mid d(p,q) \leq k\text{-}distance(p) \}$. These objects q are called the k-nearest neighbors of p.

As no confusion arises, the notation can be simplified to use $N_k(p)$ as a shorthand for $N_{k\text{-}distance(p)}(p)$.

Definition 3 (reachability distance of an object p w.r.t. object o): Let k be a natural number. The reachability distance of object p with respect to object o is defined as

$reach\text{-}dist_k(p,o)=max \{ k\text{-}distance(o), d(p,o) \}$

Definition 4 (local reachability density of an object p): The local reachability density of p is defined as

$$LRD_{MinPts}(p)=1/\left(\frac{\sum_{o \in N_{MinPts}(p)} reach-dist_{MinPts}(p,o))}{|N_{MinPts}(p)|} \right)$$

Intuitively, the local reachability density of an object p is the inverse of the average reachability distance based on the $MinPts$-nearest neighbors of p.

Definition 5 (local outlier factor of an object p): The local outlier factor of p is defined as

$$LOF_{MinPts}(p)=\frac{\sum_{o \in N_{MinPts}(p)} \frac{LRD_{MinPts}(o)}{LRD_{MinPts}(p)}}{|N_{MinPts}(p)|}$$

The LOF of object p is the average of the ratio of the LRD of p and those of p's $MinPts$-nearest neighbors. It captures the degree to which p is called an outlier. It is easy to see that the higher the ratio of the LRD of p to those of p's $MinPts$-nearest neighors is, the farther away the point p is from its nearest cluster, and the higher the LOF value of p is. Since the LOF represents the degree the object is being outlying and the LOF of most objects in a cluster is approximately equal to 1, we regard object p belong to a certain cluster if $LOF(p)$ is lower than a threshold we set.

2.1.3 A local-density based notion of clusters

When looking at the sample set of points depicted in Figure 2, we can easily and unambiguously detect clusters of points and noise points not belonging to any of those clusters. The main reason is that within each cluster the local density of points are different from that of the outside part.

In the following, these intuitive notions of "clusters" and "noise" are formalized. Note that both notion of clusters and the algorithm LDBSCAN apply to 2D Euclidean space as to higher dimensional feature space. The key idea is that for any point p satisfying $LOF(p) \leq LOFUB$, i.e. point p is not an outlier and belongs to a certain cluster C, if point q is the $MinPts$-nearest neighbour of p and has the similar LRD with p, q belongs to the same cluster C of p. This approach works with any distance function so that an appropriate function can be chosen for a given application. In this chapter, for the purpose of proper visualization, related examples will be in 2D space using the Euclidean distance.

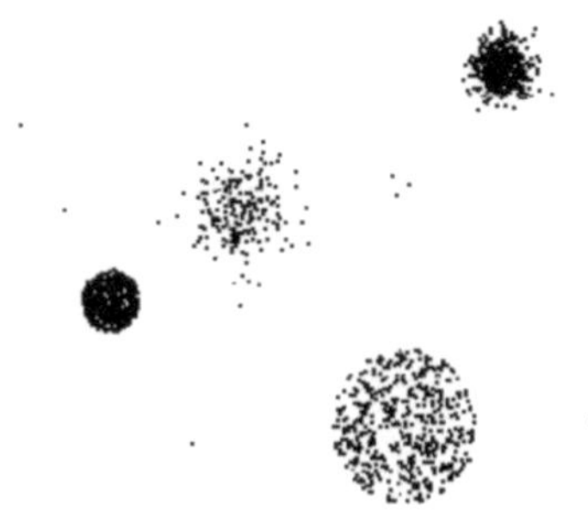

Fig. 2. Sample Data (Breunig et al., 2000)

Definition 6 (core point): A point p is a core point w.r.t. *LOFUB* if $LOF(p) \leq LOFUB$.

If $LOF(p)$ is small enough, it means that point p is not an outlier and must belong to some clusters. Therefore it can be regarded as a core point.

Definition 7 (directly local-density-reachable): A point p is directly local-density-reachable from a point q w.r.t. *pct* and *MinPts* if

1. $p \in N_{MinPts}(q)$ and
2. $LRD(q)/(1+pct) < LRD(p) < LRD(q)*(1+pct)$

Here, the parameter *pct* is used to control the fluctuation of local-density. However, in general, it is not symmetric if q is not the *MinPts*-nearest neighbour of p. Figure 3 shows the asymmetric case. Let $MinPts=3$ and $pct=0.3$, we calculate that $LRD(p)/LRD(q)=1.27$. It shows that p is directly local-density-reachable from q, but q is not directly local-density-reachable from p.

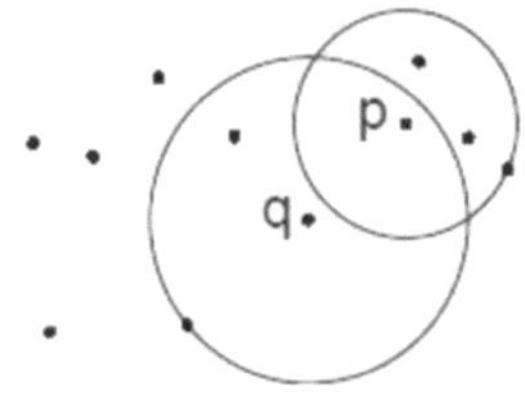

Fig. 3. Directly local-density-reachability

Definition 8 (local-density-reachable): A point p is local-density-reachable from the point q w.r.t. *pct* and *MinPts* if there is a chain of points $p_1, p_2, ..., p_n, p_1=q, p_n=p$ such that p_{i+1} is directly local-density-reachable from p_i.

Local-density-reachability is a canonical extension of direct local-density-reachability. This relation is transitive, but it is not symmetric. Figure 4 depicts the relations of some sample points and an asymmetric case. Let $MinPts=3$, $pct=0.3$. According to the above definitions, $LRD(p)/LRD(o)=1.27$, $LRD(o)/LRD(q)=0.95$. Here, q is local-density-reachable from p, but p is not local-density-reachable from q.

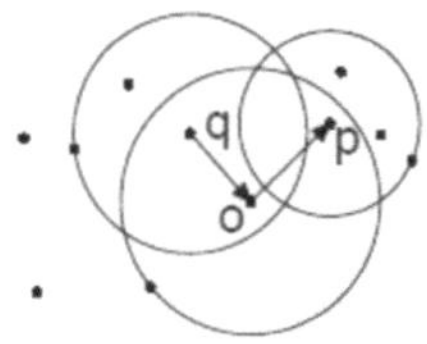

Fig. 4. Local-density-reachability

Definition 9 (local-density-connected): A point *p* is local-density-connected to a point *q* from *o* w.r.t. *pct* and *MinPts* if there is a point *o* such that both *p* and *q* are local-density-reachable from *o* w.r.t. *pct* and *MinPts*.

From the definition, local-density-connectivity is a symmetric relation show in Figure 5. Now we can make use of the above definitions to define the local-density-based cluster. Intuitively, a cluster is defined as a set of local-density-connected points which is maximal w.r.t local-density-reachability. Noised are defined relatively to a given set of clusters. Noises are simply the set of points in the dataset not belonging to any of its clusters.

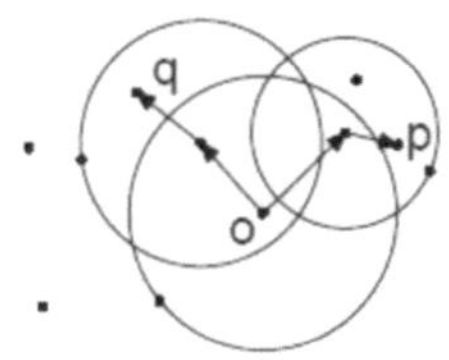

Fig. 5. Local-density-connectivity

Definition 10 (cluster): Let *D* be a database of points, and point *o* is a selected core point of *C*, i.e. $o \in C$ and $LOF(o) \leq LOFUB$. A cluster *C* w.r.t. *LOFUB*, *pct* and *MinPts* is a non-empty subset of *D* satisfying the following conditions:

1. $\forall p$: *p* is local-density-reachable from *o* w.r.t. *pct* and *MinPts*, then $p \in C$. (Maximality)
2. $\forall p,q \in C$: *p* is local-density-connected *q* by *o* w.r.t. *LOFUB*, *pct* and *MinPts*. (Connectivity)

Definition 11 (noise): Let $C_1, \ldots, C_k$ be the clusters of the database *D* w.r.t. parameters *LOFUB*, *pct* and *MinPts*. Then we define the noise as the set of points in the database *D* not belonging to any cluster C_i, i.e. noise= $\{ p \in D \mid \forall i: p \text{ not in } C_i \}$.

2.2 The algorithm

In this section, we present the algorithm LDBSCAN which is designed to discover the clusters and the noise in a spatial database according to Definition 10 and 11. First, the appropriate parameters *LOFUB*, *pct*, and *MinPts* of clusters and one core point of the respective cluster are selected. Then all points that are local-density-reachable from the given core point using the correct parameters are retrieved. Since all the parameters are relative, and not absolute as those in DBSCAN, they are easy to choose and fall in a certain range as presented in the experimental part.

To find a cluster, LDBSCAN starts with an arbitrary point *p* and retrieves all points local-density-reachable from *p* w.r.t. *LOFUB*, *pct*, and *MinPts*. If *p* is a core point, this procedure yields a cluster w.r.t *LOFUB*, *pct*, and *MinPts*. If *p* is not a core point, LDBSCAN will check the next point of the dataset. In the following, we present a basic version of LDBSCAN without details of data types and generation of additional information about clusters:

```
LDBSCAN (SetOfPoints, LOFUB, pct, MinPts)
 // SetOfPoints is UNCLASSIFIED
 InitSet (SetOfPoints); // calculate LRD and LOF of each point
 ClusterID := 0;
 FOR i FROM 1 TO SetOfPoints.size DO
  Point := SetOfPoints.get(i);
  IF Point.ClId = UNCLASSIFIED THEN
   IF LOF(Point) ≤ LOFUB THEN // core point
    ClusterID := ClusterID + 1;
    ExpandCluster(SetOfPoints, Point, ClusterID, pct, MinPts);
   ELSE // no core point
    SetOfPoint.changeClId(Point,NOISE);
   END IF
  END IF
 END FOR
END; //LDBSCAN
```

SetOfPoints is the set of the whole database. *LOFUB*, *pct* and *MinPts* are the carefully chosen parameters. The function SetOfPoints.get(i) returns the *i*-th element of SetOfPoints. Points which have been marked to be NOISE may be changed later if they are local-density-reachable from some core points of the database. The most important function used by LDBSCAN is ExpandCluster which is presented in the following:

```
ExpandCluster(SetOfPoints, Point, ClusterID, pct, MinPts)
 SetOfPoint.changeClId(Point,ClusterID);
 FOR i FROM 1 TO MinPts DO
  currentP := Point.Neighbor(i);
  IF currentP.ClId IN {UNCLASSIFIED,NOISE} and DirectReachability(currentP,Point)
THEN
   TempVector.add(currentP);
   SetOfPoint.changeClId(currentP,ClusterID);
  END IF
 END FOR
 WHILE TempVector <> Empty DO
  Point := TempVector.firstElement();
  TempVector.remove(Point);
  FOR i FROM 1 TO MinPts DO
   currentP := Point.Neighbor(i);
   IF currentP.ClId IN {UNCLASSIFIED,NOISE} and DirectReachability(currentP,Point)
THEN
    TempVector.add(currentP);
    SetOfPoint.changeClId(currentP,ClusterID);
   END IF
  END FOR
```

```
  END WHILE
END; //ExpandCluster
```

The function DirectReachability(currentP,Point) is presented in the following:

```
DirectReachability(currentP,Point) : Boolean
  IF LRD(currentP)>LRD(Point)/(1+pct) and LRD(currentP)<LRD(Point)*(1+pct) THEN
    RETURN True;
  ELSE
    RETURN False;
END; //DirectReachability
```

The LDBSCAN algorithm randomly selects one core point which has not been clustered, and then retrieves all points that are local-density-reachable from the chosen core point to form a cluster. It won't stop until there is no unclustered core point.

3. Cluster-Based Outliers

In this section, we give the definition of cluster-based outliers and conduct a detailed analysis on the properties of cluster-based outliers. The goal is to show how to discover cluster-based outliers and how the definition of the cluster-based outlier factor (CBOF) captures the spirit of cluster-based outliers. The higher the CBOF is, the more abnormal the cluster-based outliers are.

3.1 Definition of Cluster-Based Outliers

Intuitively, most data points in the data set should not be outliers; therefore, only the clusters that hold a small portion of data points are candidates for cluster-based outliers. Considering the different and complicated situations, it is impossible to provide a definite number as the upper bound of the number of the objects contained in a cluster-based outlier (UBCBO). Here, only a guideline is provided to find the reasonable upper bound.

Definition 12 (Upper Bound of the Cluster-Based Outlier): Let $C_1, ..., C_k$ be the clusters of the database D discovered by LDBSCAN in the sequence that $|C_1|\geq|C_2|\geq\ldots\geq|C_k|$. Given parameters a, the number of the objects in the cluster C_i is the *UBCBO* if $(|C_1|+|C_2|+\ldots+|C_{i-1}|)\geq|D|*a$ and $(|C_1|+|C_2|+\ldots+|C_{i-2}|)<|D|*a$.

Definition 12 gives quantitative measure to *UBCBO*. Consider that most data points in the dataset are not outliers; therefore, clusters that hold a large portion of data points should not be considered as outliers. For example, if a is set to 90%, we intend to regard clusters which contain 90% of data points as normal clusters.

Definition 13 (Cluster-based outlier): Let $C_1, ..., C_k$ be the clusters of the database D discovered by LDBSCAN. Cluster-based outliers are the clusters in which the number of the objects is no more than *UBCBO*.

Note that this guideline is not always appropriate. For example, in some cases the abnormal cluster deviated from a large cluster might contain more points than a certain small normal cluster. In fact, due to spatial and temporal locality, it would be more proper to choose the clusters which have small spatial or temporal span as cluster-based outliers than the clusters which contain few objects. The notion of cluster-based outliers depends on situations.

3.2 The lower bound of the number of objects contained in a cluster

Comparing with single point outliers, cluster-based outliers are more interesting. Many single point outliers are related to occasional trivial events, while cluster-based outliers concern some important lasting abnormal events. Generally speaking, it is reckless to form a cluster with only 2 or 3 objects, so the lower bound of the number of the objects contained in a cluster generated by LDBSCAN will be discussed in the following.

Definition 14 (distance between two clusters): Let C_1, C_2 be the clusters of the database D. The distance between C_1 and C_2 is defined as

$dist(C_1, C_2)=min\{ dist(p,q) \mid p \in C_1, q \in C_2\}$

Theorem 1: Let C_1 be the smallest cluster discovered by LDBSCAN w.r.t. appropriate parameters *LOFUB*, *pct* and *MinPts*, and C_2 is large enough be the closest normal cluster to C_1. Let $LRD(C_1)$ denote the minimum LRD of all the objects in C_1, i.e., $LRD(C_1)=min\{LRD(p) \mid p \in C_1\}$. Similarly, let $LRD(C_2)$ denote the minimum LRD of all the objects in C_2. Then for *LBC*, the lower bound of the number of the objects contained in a cluster, such that:

$$\mathrm{LBC} = [\frac{(MinPts+1)LRD(q) - (LOFUB * MinPts+1)LRD(p)}{LRD(q) - LRD(p)}] + 1$$

Proof (Sketch): Let p_i denote the *i*-th object in C_1 and $q_{i,j}$ be the *j*-th close object to p_i in C_2. And let *k* be the number of the objects in C_1. To simplify our proof, we only consider the situation that each point only has *k* *k*-nearest neighbors and the density within a cluster fluctuates slightly.

If $k \geq MinPts+1$, according to the definition of LOF, the LOF of any object in C_1 is approximately equal to 1. That is, $LOF(p_i)<LOFUB$ and each object in C_1 is a core point. In addition, each object in C_1 has the similar *LRD* to its neighbors which belong to the same cluster with it. According to the definition of the cluster, the cluster C_1 would be discovered by LDBSCAN. Thus, *LBC* is no more than $MinPts+1$.

If $k \leq MinPts$, the *MinPts*-distance neighbors of p_i contain the $k-1$ rest objects in C_1 and the other $MinPts-k+1$ neighbors in C_2 shown in Figure 6. Obviously, the *MinPts*-distance of each fixed object p_j in C_1 is greater than the distance between any object p_i in C_1 and p_j, so $reach\text{-}dist(p_i,p_j)= MinPts\text{-}distance(p_j)$. Furthermore, the $MinPts\text{-}distance(q_{i,j}) << dist(C_1,C_2) \leq d(p_i,q_{i,j})$.

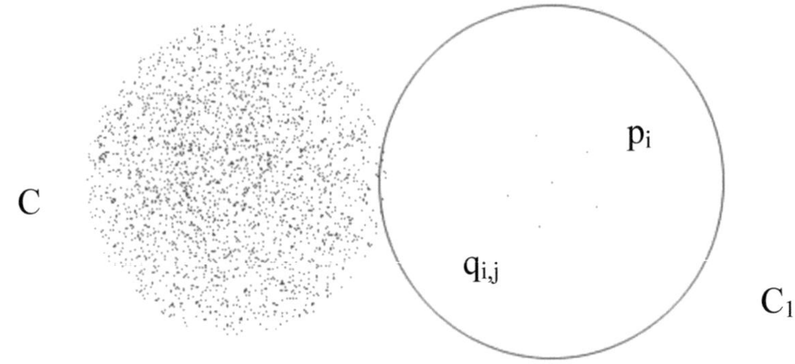

Fig. 6. 2-d Dataset

$$\Rightarrow LRD_{MinPts}(p_i) =$$
$$= MinPts / (\sum_{a=1}^{k} MinPts - dist(p_a) - MinPts - dist(p_i) + \sum_{a=1}^{MinPts-k+1} d(p_i, q_{i,a})) \quad (2)$$

and

$$LRD_{MinPts}(q_i) = MinPts / \sum_{o \in N_{MinPts}(q_i)} reach - dist_{MinPts}(q_i, o) \quad (3)$$

$\forall p_i \in C_1$: Let MinPts-dist(p)=min{MinPts-dist(p_i) | $p_i \in C_1$}, and then MinPts-dist(p_i) = MinPts-dist(p)+ε_i. Similarly, let d(p,q)=min{d(p_i,$q_{i,j}$) | $p_i \in C_1$, $q_{i,j} \in C_2$ and $q_{i,j}$ is the MinPts-neighbor of p_i} and d(p_i,$q_{i,j}$)=d(p,q)+ $\varepsilon_{i,j}$. Because we assume that the density within a cluster fluctuates slightly, MinPts-dist(p)>> ε_i and d(p,q)>> $\varepsilon_{i,j}$.

Compare the *LRD* of object p_i with that of its neighbor p_j in C_1.

$$\frac{LRD_{MinPts}(p_i)}{LRD_{MinPts}(p_j)} = \frac{\sum_{a=1}^{k} MinPts - dist(p_a) - MinPts - dist(p_j) + \sum_{a=1}^{MinPts-k+1} d(p_j, q_{j,a})}{\sum_{a=1}^{k} MinPts - dist(p_a) - MinPts - dist(p_i) + \sum_{a=1}^{MinPts-k+1} d(p_i, q_{i,a})}$$
$$= \frac{\sum_{a=1}^{k} MinPts - dist(p_a) - MinPts - dist(p) - \varepsilon_j + \sum_{a=1}^{MinPts-k+1} (d(p,q) + \varepsilon_{j,a})}{\sum_{a=1}^{k} MinPts - dist(p_a) - MinPts - dist(p) - \varepsilon_i + \sum_{a=1}^{MinPts-k+1} (d(p,q) + \varepsilon_{i,a})}$$
$$= \frac{\sum_{a=1}^{k} MinPts - dist(p_a) - MinPts - dist(p) + (MinPts - k + 1) * d(p,q) + \sum_{a=1}^{MinPts-k+1} \varepsilon_{j,a} - \varepsilon_j}{\sum_{a=1}^{k} MinPts - dist(p_a) - MinPts - dist(p) + (MinPts - k + 1) * d(p,q) + \sum_{a=1}^{MinPts-k+1} \varepsilon_{i,a} - \varepsilon_i}$$
$$\approx 1$$

Thus, the objects in C_1 have the similar LRD.

Now consider the ratio of the LRD of the object p_i to that of its neighbor q_j in C_2. Let reach-dist-max be the maximum reachability distance of the object q_j which is the object in C_2.

$\because MinPts - dist(p_i) > dist(C_1, C_2)$ and $d(p_i, q_{i,j}) > dist(C_1, C_2)$

$$\therefore \frac{LRD_{MinPts}(q_j)}{LRD_{MinPts}(p_i)} = \frac{\sum_{a=1}^{k} MinPts - dist(p_a) - MinPts - dist(p_i) + \sum_{a=1}^{MinPts-k+1} d(p_i, q_{i,a})}{\sum_{o \in N_{MinPts}(q_i)} reach - dist_{MinPts}(q_i, o)}$$
$$> \frac{MinPts * dist(C_1, C_2)}{MinPts * reach - dist - \max} = \frac{dist(C_1, C_2)}{reach - dist - \max}$$

$\because dist(C_1, C_2) >> reach-dist-\max$ and the appropriate pct<1

$\therefore \frac{LRD(q_j)}{LRD(p_i)} >> 2 > 1 + pct$. That is, objects in C2 will not be assigned to cluster C1.

Then, if objects in C_1 form a cluster which can be discovered by LDBSCAN, the inequality, $Min(LOF_{MinPts}(p_i)) \le LOFUB$, must be satisfied.

$$\Rightarrow Min(LOF_{MinPts}(p_i)) = Min(\frac{\sum_{a=1}^{k} LRD_{MinPts}(p_a) - LRD_{MinPts}(p_i) + \sum_{a=1}^{MinPts-k+1} LRD(q_{i,a})}{MinPts * LRD_{MinPts}(p_i)})$$

$$\ge \frac{(k-1)LRD(p) + (MinPts-k+1)LRD(q)}{MinPts * (LRD(p) + \varepsilon_i)}$$

$$\Rightarrow \frac{(k-1)LRD(p) + (MinPts-k+1)LRD(q)}{MinPts * (LRD(p) + \varepsilon_i)} \le LOFUB$$

$$\Rightarrow (MinPts+1)LRD(q) - LRD(p) \le LOFUB * MinPts * (LRD(p) + \varepsilon_i) + k * (LRD(q) - LRD(p))$$

$$\Rightarrow k \ge \frac{(MinPts+1)LRD(q) - (LOFUB * MinPts + 1)LRD(p) - LOFUB * MinPts * \varepsilon_i}{LRD(q) - LRD(p)}$$

$$\therefore \text{LBC} = [\frac{(MinPts+1)LRD(q) - (LOFUB * MinPts + 1)LRD(p)}{LRD(q) - LRD(p)}] + 1$$

Since the LOF of objects deep in a cluster is approximately equal to 1, the LOFUB must be greater than 1. Then

$$\text{LBC} = [\frac{(MinPts+1)LRD(q) - (LOFUB * MinPts + 1)LRD(p)}{LRD(q) - LRD(p)}] + 1$$

$$< [\frac{(MinPts+1)LRD(q) - (MinPts + 1)LRD(p)}{LRD(q) - LRD(p)}] + 1 = MinPts + 2$$

In other words, LBC satisfies the inequality, $LBC \le MinPts+1$, discussed in part (a). Let's consider another extreme situation. The LOFUB is so big that (LOFUB*MinPts+1)*LRD(p) is bigger than (MinPts+1)*LRD(q), and in this case LBC is less than 1. As a matter of fact, it is impossible for LBC to be less than 1. When LOFUB is big enough, the object p which is a single point outlier still satisfies the core point condition, $LOF(p) \le LOFUB$; therefore, the object p is deemed as a core point that should belong to a certain cluster. In this case, it forms a cluster which contains only one object by itself.

3.3 The Cluster-Based Outlier Factor

Since outliers are far more than a binary property (Breunig et al., 2000), a cluster-based outlier also needs a value to demonstrate its degree of being an outlier. In the following we give the definition of the cluster-based outlier factor.

Definition 15 (Cluster-based outlier factor): Let C_1 be a cluster-based outlier and C_2 be the nearest non-outlier cluster of C_1. The cluster-based outlier factor of C_1 is defined as

$$CBOF(C_1) = |C_1| * dist(C_1, C_2) * \sum_{p_i \in C_2} lrd(p_i) / |C_2|$$

The cluster-based outlier factor of the cluster C_1 is the result of multiplying the number of the objects in C_1 by the product of the distance between C_1 and its nearest normal cluster C_2 and the average local reachability density of C_2. The outlier factor of cluster C_1 captures the degree to which we call C_1 an outlier. Assume that C_1 as a cluster-based outlier is deviated from its nearest normal cluster C_2. It is easy to see that the more objects C_1 contains, and the farther away C_1 is from C_2, and the more dense C_2 is, the higher the *CBOF* of C_1 is and the more abnormal C_1 is.

4. Experiments

A comprehensive performance study has been conducted to evaluate our algorithm. In this section, we describe those experiments and their results. The algorithm was run on both real-life datasets obtained from the UCI Machine Learning Repository and synthetic datasets.

4.1 LDBSCAN

In this section, we will demonstrate how the proposed LDBSCAN can successfully generate clusters which appear to be meaningful that is unable to be generated by other methods.

4.1.1 A synthetic dataset with clusters resided in other clusters

In order to test the effectiveness of the algorithm, both LDBSCAN and OPTICS are applied to a data set with 473 points as shown in Figure 7. Both LDBSCAN and OPTICS can generate the magenta cluster D, the cyan cluster E, and the green cluster F. But OPTICS can only generate the cluster G which contains all the magenta, cyan, green, and pink points. And it is more reasonable to generate a cluster which only contains the pink points because of their similarity in local-density. Therefore LDBSCAN produces the similar local-density clusters instead of the clusters produced by OPTICS with local-density exceeds certain thresholds.

The result of LDBSCAN can be influenced by the choice of the parameters. There are two totally different parameters of *MinPts*. One is for the calculation of LOF and the other is for the clustering algorithm. For most of the datasets, it seems work well when *MinPts* for LOF is between 10 and 20, and more details can be found in (Breunig et al., 2000). For convenience of presentation, $MinPts_{LOF}$ is used as a shorthand of *MinPts* for LOF and $MinPts_{LDBSCAN}$ as a shorthand of *MinPts* for the clustering algorithm.

For objects deep inside a cluster, the LOFs are approximately equal to 1. The greater the LOF is, the higher possibility for the object to be an outlier. If the value that is selected for *LOFUB* is too small, some core points may be mistakenly considered as outliers; and if the value is too large, some outliers may be mistakenly considered as core points. For most of the datasets that have been experimented with, picking 1.5 to 2.5 appears to work well.

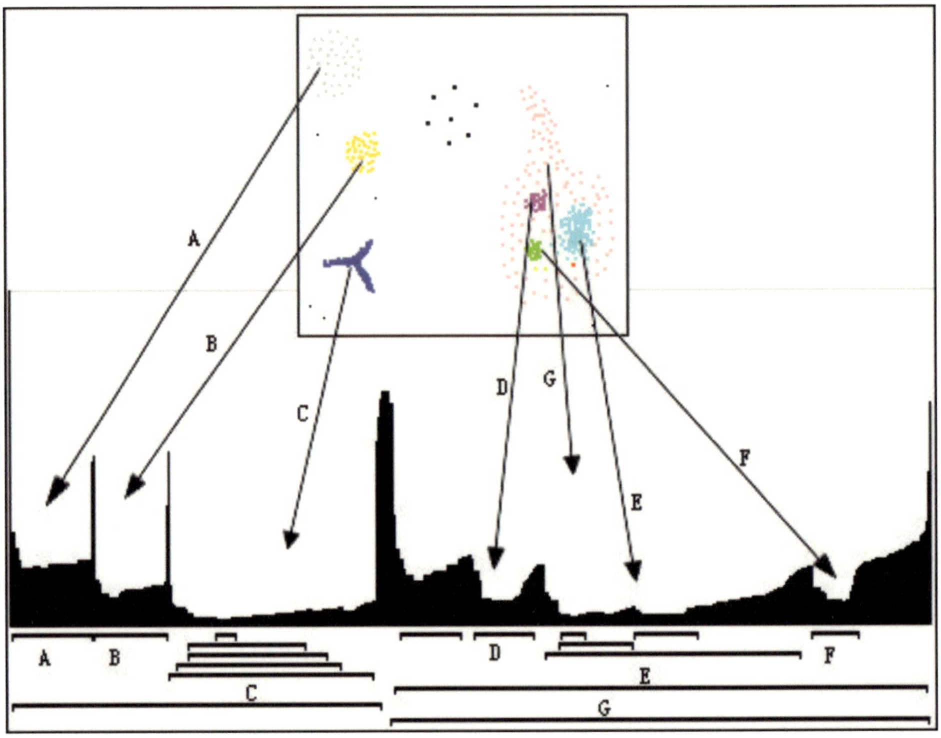

Fig. 7. Reachability-plot for a data set with hierarchical clusters of different sizes, densities and shapes

However, it also depends. For example, we identified multiple clusters, e.g., a cluster of pictures from a tennis match and the reasonable *LOFUB* is up to 7. In Figure 8, the red points are those whose LOF exceeds the *LOFUB* when $MinPts_{LOF}=15$.

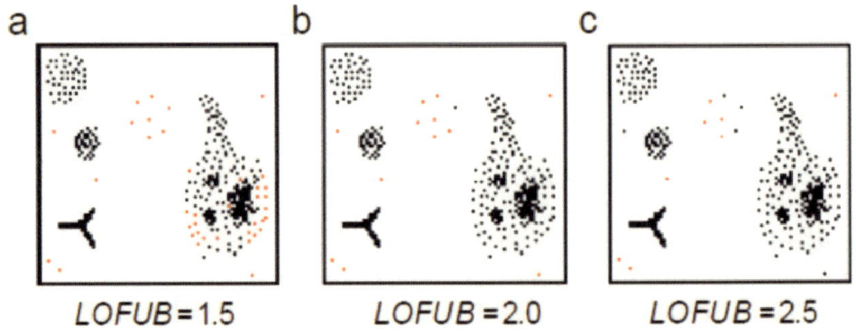

Fig. 8. Core points and outliers

Parameter *pct* controls the local-density fluctuation as it is accepted. The value of *pct* depends on the fluctuation of the cluster. Generally speaking, it is between 0.2 and 0.5. Of course in some particular situations, other values out of this range can be chosen. Let $MinPts_{LOF}=15$, $MinPts_{LDBSCAN}=10$, and $LOFUB=2.0$. Figure 9 shows the different clustering results with different values of *pct*.

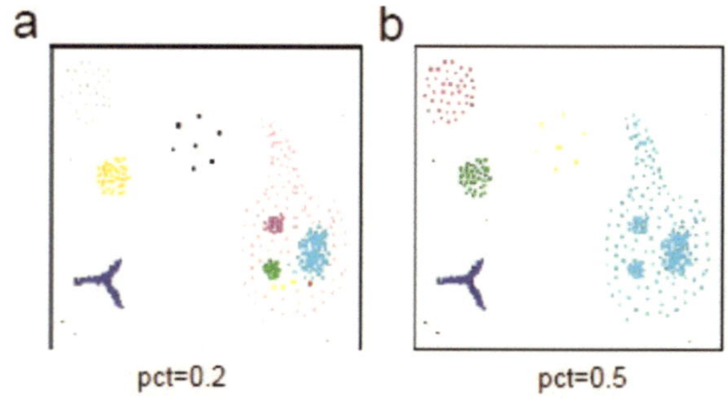

Fig. 9. Clustering results with different values of *pct*.

Parameter $MinPts_{LDBSCAN}$ determines the stand-by objects belonging to the same cluster of the core point. Clearly $MinPts_{LDBSCAN}$ can be as small as 1. However, if $MinPts_{LDBSCAN}$ is too small, some reasonable objects may be missed. Thus we suggest that $MinPts_{LDBSCAN}$ is at least 5 in order to take enough reasonable objects into account. The upper bound of $MinPts_{LDBSCAN}$ is based on a more subtle observation. Let $p \in C_1$, $q \in C_2$, C_1 has the similar density with C_2. p and q are the nearest objects between C_1 and C_2. Consider the simple situation that $distance(C_1, C_2)$ is small enough shown in Figure 10, obviously that as $MinPts_{LDBSCAN}$ values increase, there will be a corresponding monotonic sequence of changes to *MinPts-distance(p)*. As the $MinPts_{LDBSCAN}$ values increase, once *MinPts-distance(p)* is greater than $distance(C_1, C_2)$, C_1 and C_2 will be generated into one cluster. In Figure 10, clustering with any core point in C_1 is started. When $MinPts_{LDBSCAN}$ reaches 10, C_1 and C_2 will be generated into one cluster C. Therefore, the value for $MinPts_{LDBSCAN}$ should not be too large. When $MinPts_{LDBSCAN}$ reaches 15, enough candidates will be considered. The value ranges from 5 to 15 can be chosen for $MinPts_{LDBSCAN}$.

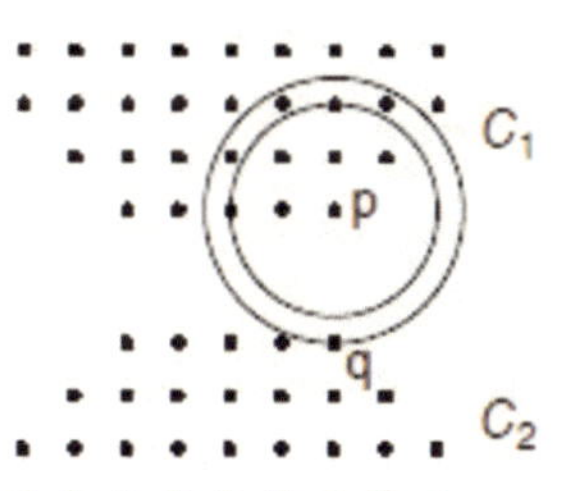

Fig. 10. Different values for $MinPts_{LDBSCAN}$.

4.1.2 Comet-like clusters

In order to demonstrate the accuracy of the clustering results of LDBSCAN, both LDBSCAN and OPTICS are applied to a 2-dimension dataset shown in the following Figure 11. LDBSCAN discovers the cluster C_1 consisting of small rectangle points, the cluster C_2 consisting of small circle points, and the outlier P_1, P_2, P_3 denoted by hollow rectangle points. OPTICS discovers the clusters whose reachability-distance falls into the dents and assigns the point to a cluster according to its reachability-distance, regardless its

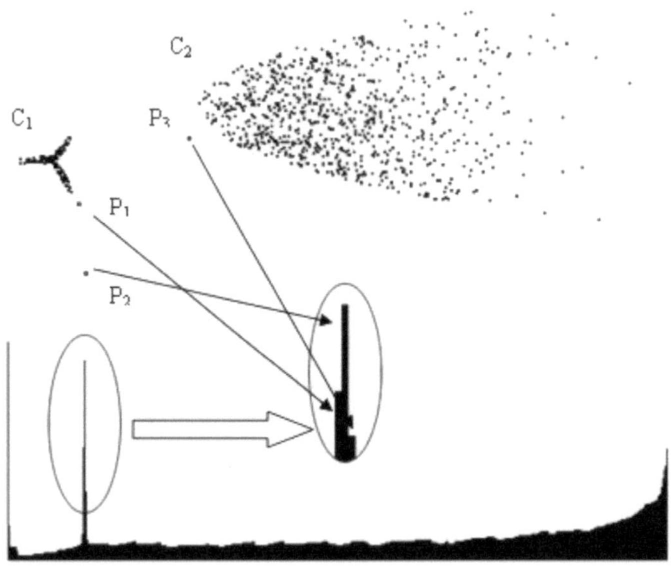

Fig. 11. Clusters with different local density borders.

neighborhood density. Because the reachability-distance of the point P_3 is similar to that of the points in the right side of the cluster C_2, the side whose density is relatively low, OPTICS would assign the point P_3 to the cluster C_2, while LDBSCAN discovers the point P_3 as an outlier due to its different local density from its neighbors. Although both OPTICS and LDBSCAN can discover the points P_1, P_2 as outliers, the clustering result of OPTICS is not accurate especially when the border density of a cluster varies, such as the comet-like cluster.

4.2 Cluster-based outliers

The performance of cluster-based outliers is tested in this section.

4.2.1 Wisconsin breast cancer data

The second used dataset is the Wisconsin breast cancer data set, which has 699 instances with nine attributes, and each record is labeled as benign (458 or 65.5%) or malignant (241 or 34.5%). In order to avoid the situation in which the local density can be ∞ if there are more than MinPts objects, different from each other, but sharing the same spatial coordinates, only 3 duplicates of certain spatial coordinates are reserved and the rest are removed. In addition, the 16 records with missing values are also removed. Therefore, the resultant dataset has 327 (57.8%) benign records and 239 (42.2%) malignant records.

The algorithm processed the dataset when *pct=0.5, LOFUB=3, MinPts=10*, and *a=0.95*. Both LOF and our algorithm find the 4 following noise records which are sing point outliers shown in Table 1. Understandably, our algorithm processes based on the result of LOF, and thus both can find the same single point outliers.

Sample code number	Value	Type	LOF
1033078	2,1,1,1,2,1,1,1,5	Benign	3.142
1177512	1,1,1,1,10,1,1,1,1	Benign	4.047
1197440	1,1,1,2,1,3,1,1,7	Benign	3.024
654546	1,1,1,1,2,1,1,1,8	Benign	4.655

Table 1. Single point outliers in Wisconsin breast cancer dataset

Besides the single point outliers, our algorithm discovers 3 clusters shown in Table 2, among which there are 2 big clusters and 1 small cluster. One big cluster A contains 296 benign records and 6 malignant records, and the other one B contains 26 benign records and 233 malignant records. The small cluster C contains only 1 record *p*. Among all the MinPts-nearest neighbors of the only one record in C, six neighbors belong to the cluster *A* and the other four belong to the cluster *B*. The record p is in the middle of cluster *A* and *B*, and *LOF(p)= 1.795*. It is closer to *A* than *B*, but has the similar local reachability density to *B* rather than *A*. Thus, it forms a cluster by itself. This kind of special record cannot be easily discovered by LOF when its *MinPts*-nearest neighborhood overlaps with more than one cluster.

Cluster Name	Number of Benign Records	Number of Malignant Records	Average Local Reachability Density
A	296	6	0.743
B	26	233	0.167
C	1	0	0.170

Table 2. Clusters in Wisconsin breast cancer dataset

4.2.2 Boston housing data

The Boston housing dataset, which is taken from the StatLib library, concerns housing values in suburbs of Boston. It contains 506 instances with 14 attributes. Before clustering, data need to be standardized in order to assign each variable an equal weight. Here the z-score process is used because using mean absolute deviation is more robust than using standard deviation (Han & Kamber, 2006). The algorithm processed the dataset when *pct=0.5, LOFUB=2, MinPts=10,* and *a=0.9*. One single point outlier, 3 normal clusters and 6 cluster-based outliers are discovered. There are few single point outliers in this dataset. The maximum LOF, the value of the 381st record, is 2.624 which indicates that there is not a significant deviation. In addition, the 381st record is assigned to the 9th cluster which is a cluster-based outlier. Its LOF exceeds *LOFUB* due to the small number of the objects contained in the 9th cluster to which it belongs. The small number, which is less than *MinPts*, would affect the accuracy of LOF. Eight of all the nine records whose LOF exceeds *LOFUB* are assigned to a certain cluster and the LOF of the only single point outlier, the 215th record, is 2.116. The 215th record has a smaller proportion of owner-occupied units built prior to 1940, the 7th attribute, than its neighbors.

However, the 6 cluster-based outliers are more interesting than the only single point outlier. Table 3 demonstrates the information of all the 9 clusters, and the additional information of the cluster-based outliers is shown in Table 4. The 3rd cluster, which is a cluster-based outlier and has the maximum CBOF, deviates from the 1st cluster. Its 12th attribute, $1000(Bk - 0.63)^2$ where Bk is the proportion of blacks by town, is much lower than that of the 1st cluster. Both the 9th cluster and the 6th cluster deviate from the 1st cluster. Although the 6th cluster contains more object than the 9th cluster, the CBOF of the 6th cluster is less than that of the 9th cluster because the 9th cluster is farther away from the 1st cluster than the 6th cluster. The records in the 9th cluster have significantly big per capita crime rate by town, comparing with those of the 1st cluster. However, it is not easy to do not differentiate the records in the 6th cluster from those of the 1st cluster. Moreover, the relationship between the 4th cluster and the 8th cluster is also impressive. There are 35 records which show that its tract bounds the Charles River, demonstrated by the 4th attribute, in the whole dataset,

Cluster Id	Number of Records	Average Local Reachability Density
1	82	0.556
2	345	0.528
3	26	0.477
4	34	0.266
5	1	0.303
6	9	0.228
7	1	0.228
8	1	0.155
9	6	0.127

Table 3. Clusters in Boston housing dataset

Cluster Id	CBOF	Nearest cluster	dist(C1, C2)	The nearest object pair	The contained records
3	54.094	1	3.744	436--445	412,416,417,420,424,425, 426,427,429,430,431,432, 433,434,435,436,437,438, 439,446,451,455,456,457, 458,467
9	24.514	1	7.353	415--385	381,406,411,415,419, 428
6	20.005	1	4.000	399--401	366,368,369,372,399, 405,413,414,418
7	2.452	2	4.648	103--35	103
5	2.269	1	4.084	410--461	410
8	1.468	4	5.522	284--283	284

Table 4. Cluster-based outliers in Boston housing dataset

and 34 of them is discovered in the 4th cluster. The only exceptional record, the 284th record, has a slightly high proportion of residential land zoned for lots over 25,000 square feet, the 2nd attribute, and a relatively low proportion of non-retail business acres per town, the 3rd attribute. The area denoted by the 284th record is more like a residential area than the other areas along the Charles River.

5. Conclusion

In this chapter, we have examined various density-based techniques, DBSCAN, OPTICS, LOF, LDBSCAN and cluster-based outlier detection, and have described several applications of these techniques. Clustering is a process of grouping data based on a measure of similarity, and outlier detection is a process of discovering the data objects which are grossly different from or inconsistent with the remaining set of data. Both clustering and outlier detection is a subjective process; the same set of data often needs to be processed differently for different applications. This subjectivity makes the process of clustering and outlier detection hard. That is why a single algorithm or approach is not adequate to solve all the problems.

The most challenging step is feature extraction and pattern representation. In this chapter, the step of pattern representation is conveniently avoided by assuming the pattern representations are available as input to the clustering and outlier detection algorithm. Especially in the case of large data sets, it is difficult for the user to keep track of the importance of each feature. Comparing with partitioning and hierarchical methods, density-based methods stand out both in discovering clusters with arbitrary shape and in outlier detection. Among them, the OPTICS and LDBSCAN are most successful used due to their accuracy. They can effectively discover clusters with different local density. In summary, clustering and outlier detection is an interesting, useful and challenging problem. Density-based techniques are good at accuracy; however, the potential can only be exploited after making several designed choices carefully.

6. References

Ankerst, M.; Breunig, M. M. ; Kriegel, H.-P. & Sander, J. (1999). OPTICS: ordering points to identify the clustering structure. In Proceedings of the 1999 ACM SIGMOD international conference on Management of data (SIGMOD '99). ACM, New York, NY, USA, 49-60.

Breunig, M. M. ; Kriegel, H.-P. ; Ng, R. T. & Sander, J. (2000), LOF: identifying density-based local outliers, Proceedings of the 2000 ACM SIGMOD international conference on Management of data, p.93-104, May 15-18, 2000, Dallas, Texas, United States.

Duan, L. ; Xu, L. ; Guo, F. ; Lee, J. & Yan, B. (2007). A local-density based spatial clustering algorithm with noise. Inf. Syst. 32, 7 (November 2007), 978-986.

Duan, L. ; Xu, L. ; Liu, Y. & Lee, J. (2009). Cluster-based Outlier Detection. Annals of Operations Research. Vol 168, No. 1, pp. 151-168.

Ester, M. ; Kriegel, H.-P. ; Sander, J. & Xu, X. (1996). A density-based algorithm for discovering clusters in large spatial databases with noise. In: Simoudis, E., Han, J., Fayyad, U.M. (Eds.), Proceedings of the Second International Conference on Knowledge Discovery and Data Mining, AAAI, Menlo Park, CA. pp. 226-231.

Guha, S.; Rastogi, R. & Shim, K. (1998). CURE: an efficient clustering algorithm for large databases. In Proceedings of the 1998 ACM SIGMOD international conference on Management of data (SIGMOD '98), Ashutosh Tiwary and Michael Franklin (Eds.). ACM, New York, NY, USA, 73-84.

Han, J., and Kamber, M. (2006). Data Mining: Concepts and Techniques. Elsevier.

Hinneburg, A. & Keim, D. A. (1998). An Efficient Approach to Clustering in Large Multimedia Databases with Noise. In Proc. 4th Int. Conf. on Knowledge Discovery and Data Mining, New York, NY, pp. 58-65.

Kaufman, L.; Rousseeuw, P. J. (1990). Finding Groups in Data: An Introduction to Cluster Analysis. New York: John Wiley & Sons.

MacQueen, J. (1967). Some methods for classification and analysis of multivariate observations. Proc. 5th Berkeley Symp. Math. Statist, Prob., 1: 281-297.

6

Data Mining Based on Neural Networks for Gridded Rainfall Forecasting

Kavita Pabreja
Birla Institute of Technology and Science,
Pilani, Rajasthan,
Maharaja Surajmal Institute (GGSIP University),
New Delhi,
India

1. Introduction

The application of neural networks in the data mining has become wider. Although neural networks may have complex structure and long training time but they have high acceptance ability for noisy data and high accuracy. Artificial neural network (ANN), has emerged during last decade as an analysis and forecasting tool in the field of weather. In this chapter the data mining based on neural networks has been used to forecast daily rainfall over Indian region. ANN has been trained for forecasting the rainfall of current year based on previous year's rainfall for the months of June to September. The ANN hence trained has demonstrated promising results.

2. Literature review

ANN has been applied in a few weather forecasting cases in the past. A neural network, using input from the Eta Model and upper air soundings, has been developed by Hall et al.,1999 for the probability of precipitation (PoP) and quantitative precipitation forecast (QPF) for the Dallas–Fort Worth, Texas, area. Forecasts from two years were verified against a network of 36 rain gauges. The resulting forecasts were remarkably sharp, with over 70% of the PoP forecasts being less than 5% or greater than 95%.

A neuro-fuzzy system has been used for rainfall forecasting using data from 1893-1933 as training set and 1934-1980 as test set. ANN has shown outstanding forecasting performance in many other weather related forecasts (Hayati & Mohebi, 2007; Chattopadhyay, 2007; Paras et al., 2007; Collins & Tissot, 2008). In this chapter, we have tried to forecast rainfall based on only the latitude and longitude of previous year's rainfall datasets and the results were found to be very convincing.

3. About artificial neural network

An ANN is a mathematical model or computational model that is inspired by the structure and/or functional aspects of biological neural networks. A neural network consists of an interconnected group of artificial neurons, and it processes information using a connectionist approach to computation (Sivanandam et al., 2009). In most cases an ANN is an adaptive system that changes its structure based on external or internal information that flows through the network during the learning phase. Modern neural networks are non-linear statistical data modeling tools. They are usually used to model complex relationships between inputs and outputs or to find patterns in data. An ANN is configured for a specific application, such as pattern recognition or data classification, through a learning process. For the configuration, there are network functions used for training and testing of the network, as explained in following sections.

3.1 Network function

The word '*network*'' refers to the inter-connections between the neurons in the different layers of each system. The most basic system has three layers. The first layer has input neurons which send data via synapses to the second layer of neurons and then via more synapses to the third layer of output neurons. More complex systems have more layers of neurons with some having increased layers of input neurons and output neurons. The synapses store parameters called "weights" which are used to manipulate the data in the calculations.

The layers network through the mathematics of the system algorithms. The network function $f(x)$ is defined as a composition of other functions $g_i(x)$, which can further be defined as a composition of other functions. This can be conveniently represented as a network structure, with arrows depicting the dependencies between variables, as shown in Fig. 1.

3.2 Training and testing the network

In an Artificial Neural Network, the system parameters are changed during operation, normally called the training phase. After the training phase, the Artificial Neural Network parameters are fixed and the system is deployed to solve the problem at hand (the testing phase). The Artificial Neural Network is built with a systematic step-by-step procedure to optimize a performance criterion or to follow some implicit internal constraint, which is commonly referred to as the learning rule (Kosko, 2005). The input/output training data are fundamental in neural network technology, because they convey the necessary information to "discover" the optimal operating point. The nonlinear nature of the neural network processing elements (PEs) provides the system with lots of flexibility to achieve practically any desired input/output map, i.e., some Artificial Neural Networks are universal mappers.

An input is presented to the neural network and a corresponding desired or target response set at the output (when this is the case the training is called supervised). An error is composed from the difference between the desired response and the system output. This error information is fed back to the system and adjusts the system parameters in a systematic fashion (the learning rule). The process is repeated until the performance is acceptable. It is clear from this description that the performance hinges heavily on the data. If one does not have data that cover a significant portion of the operating conditions or if they are noisy, then neural network technology is probably not the right solution. On the other hand, if there is plenty of data and the problem is poorly understood to derive an approximate model, then neural network technology is a good choice. In artificial neural networks, the designer chooses the network topology, the performance function, the learning rule, and the criterion to stop the training phase, but the system automatically adjusts the parameters. So, it is difficult to bring a priori information into the design, and when the system does not work properly it is also hard to incrementally refine the solution. But ANN-based solutions are extremely efficient in terms of development time and resources, and in many difficult problems artificial neural networks provide performance that is difficult to match with other technologies.

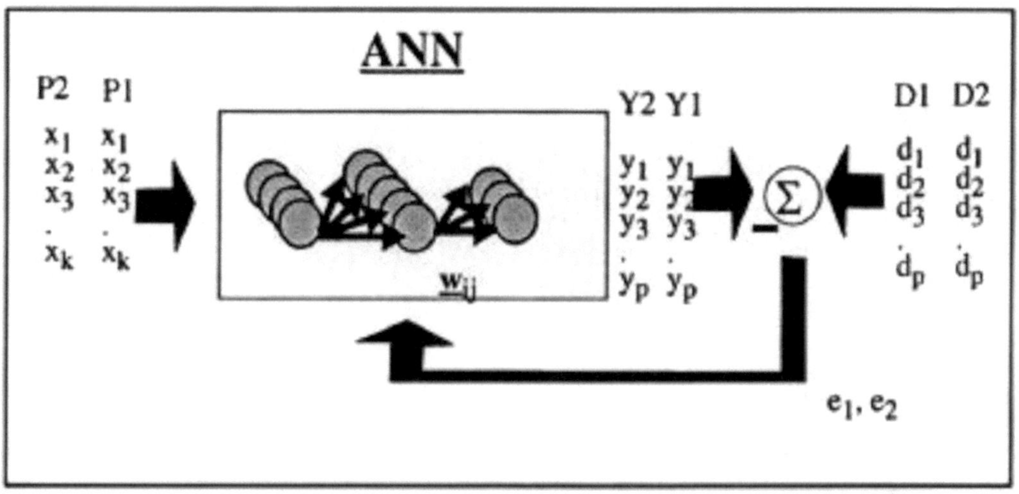

Fig. 1. Style of neural computation

3.3 MLP back propagation network

This is the most common neural network model, also known as supervised network because it requires a desired output in order to learn. The goal of this type of network is to create a model that correctly maps the input to the output using the historical data so that the model then can be used to produce the output when the desired output is unknown.

In this network, shown in Fig. 2, the input data are fed to input nodes and then they will pass to the hidden nodes after multiplying by a weight. A hidden layer adds up the weighted input received from the input nodes, associates it with the bias and then passes the result on through a nonlinear transfer function. The output node does the same operation as that of a hidden layer. This type of network is preferred as back propagation learning is a popular algorithm to adjust the interconnection weights during training, based upon the generalized delta rule proposed (Kosko, 2005).

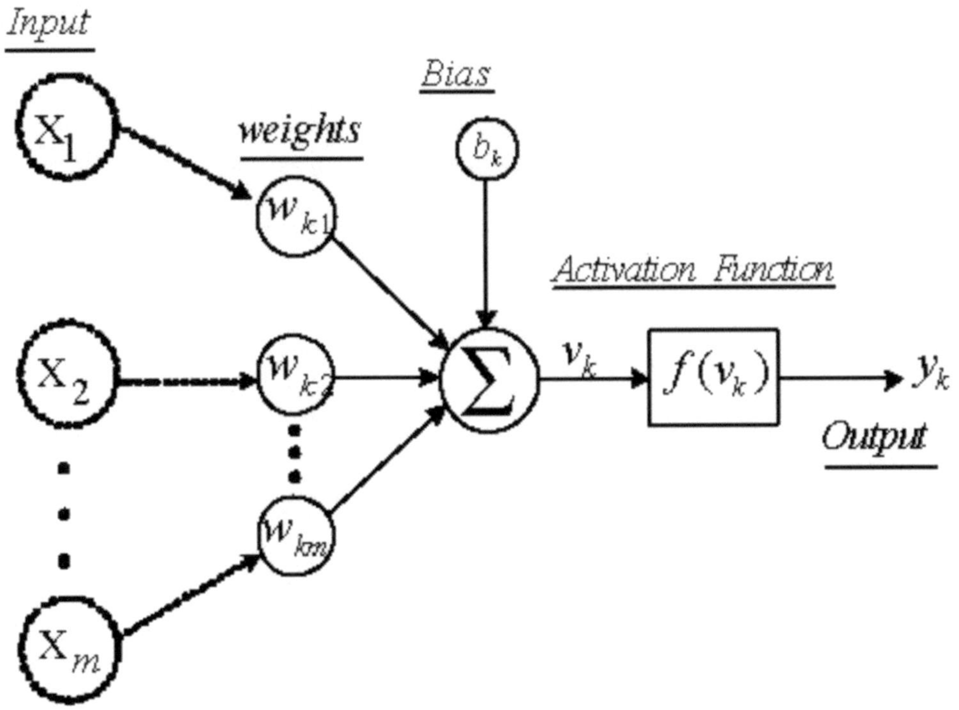

Fig. 2. Neuron Model

4. Case study of rainfall forecasting

4.1 Datasets used

A very high resolution (0.5° × 0.5°) daily rainfall (in mm) dataset for mesoscale meteorological studies over the Indian region has been provided by Indian Meteorological Department (IMD) and described by Rajeevan & Bhate(2009). The dataset is in .grd format, a control file describing the structure of .grd file has been provided. There is one .grd file for each year of rainfall.

This dataset consists of daily rainfall data for each year for the period 1984–2003. The data is for the geographical region from longitude 66.5 °E to 100.5 °E and latitude 6.5 °N to 38.5 °N for each day of the year. There are 4485 grid points readings every day and rainfall record for 122 days (June to September) per year are selected for analysis i.e 5,47,170 records out of a total of 16,37,025 records for one year of rainfall.

4.2 Data re-processing

Steps followed for pre-processing of the .grd so that the ANN can be trained and tested, are mentioned below:

1. The .grd file has been converted to .dat file using a FORTRAN (Formula Translator) programme. This dataset is very huge in size.
2. The .txt files have been exported to Excel worksheet and then to Access database. The data looks like as if a rectangular grid is filled with values of rainfall in mm.(a sample of year 1989 rainfall is shown in table 1).
3. A programme is written in Visual Basic so as to organize data in tabular format with rainfall mentioned at every grid point on each day, as shown in table 2.
4. Finally exporting the dataset into .xls format for analysis, by Matlab (Matrix Laboratory).

The daily rainfall dataset taken into consideration for the training of Neural Network is from longitude 70.5 °E to 90.0 °E and latitude 17.5°N to 37.0°N for the time period June to September for the years 1989 to 1992 as the focus is on Indian subcontinent only.

Longitude (°E)

Latitude(°N)	75	75.5	76	76.5	77	77.5	78	78.5	79	79.5
38.5	-999	-999	-999	-999	-999	-999	-999	-999	-999	-999
38	-999	-999	-999	-999	-999	-999	-999	-999	-999	-999
37.5	-999	-999	-999	-999	-999	-999	-999	-999	-999	-999
37	-999	-999	-999	-999	0	0	0	-999	-999	-999
36.5	-999	-999	-999	-999	4.4	1.2	0	-999	-999	-999
36	-999	-999	-999	9.8	8	1.5	0	1	-999	-999
35.5	-999	-999	-999	6.4	6.5	1	7.3	2.8	-999	-999
35	-999	-999	7.7	7.4	24.2	11.7	17.3	24.2	2	-999
34.5	-999	-999	7.1	10.7	6.2	7.1	27.8	16.2	10.6	5.8
34	-999	-999	0.4	16	0.3	1.8	0.8	7.7	7.9	0
33.5	-999	45.5	0	23.5	37.3	5.2	13.6	1.8	0	0
33	10.6	0.3	15	27.9	17	0	0	0	4.7	1.1
32.5	0	0	1.8	31.2	8.3	5.9	0.3	7.7	3.6	3.7
32	0	14.4	24.9	9.3	0	0	0.4	0	2.7	0
31.5	0	1.6	0.2	3.4	0	1.5	0	0	2.2	0
31	0	0	6	1.7	0	0	0	0	5	1.6
30.5	2.4	2.2	4.2	0	0	0	1.6	0	0	0

(Source: as a result of pre-processing rf1989.grd provided by IMD)

Table 1. Text file retrieved from .grd file for rainfall in 1989

Table1989					
S.No.	Day#	Date	Latitude (°N)	Longitude (°E)	Rainfall (in mm)
404	1	01-Jun-89	34.5	76	7.1
405	1	01-Jun-89	34.5	76.5	10.7
406	1	01-Jun-89	34.5	77	6.2
407	1	01-Jun-89	34.5	77.5	7.1
408	1	01-Jun-89	34.5	78	27.8
409	1	01-Jun-89	34.5	78.5	16.2
410	1	01-Jun-89	34.5	79	10.6
411	1	01-Jun-89	34.5	79.5	5.8

(Source: as a result of pre-processing rf1989.grd provided by IMD)

Table 2. Rainfall for year 1989 organized in tabular format

4.3 Technique used

ANN in this study was trained and simulated using Matlab 7.0 (matrix laboratory) designed and developed by Math Works Inc. For the training and testing of network, a two layer MLP

Day no.	Latitude	Longitude	Rainfall
1	35.5	76.5	6.4
1	35.5	77	6.5
1	35.5	77.5	1
1	35.5	78	7.3
1	35.5	78.5	2.8
1	35	76	7.7
1	35	76.5	7.4
1	35	77	24.2
1	35	77.5	11.7
1	35	78	17.3
1	35	78.5	24.2
1	35	79	2
1	34.5	76	7.1
1	34.5	76.5	10.7
1	34.5	77	6.2
1	34.5	77.5	7.1

(Source: as a result of pre-processing rf1989.grd provided by IMD)

Table 3. Sample of location-wise rainfall for year 1989

Back Propagation network has been used. The input dataset comprises of daynumber (day 1 corresponds to June 1, day 2 to June 2 and so on till day number 122 that corresponds to September 30), latitude and longitude. The output data corresponds to rainfall in mm. A sample of dataset is shown in table 3. From this table, columns 1 to 3 are used as input and column 4 is used as target.

Before training, the inputs and outputs have been scaled so that they fall in the range[-1,1]. The following code has been used at Matlab prompt:-

```
[pn1992,minp,maxp,tn1992,mint,maxt]=premnmx(linput,loutput)
```

The original network inputs and targets are given in the matrices linput and loutput. The normalized inputs and targets, pn1992 and tn1992, that are returned, will all fall in the interval [-1,1]. The vectors minp and maxp contain the minimum and maximum values of the original inputs, and the vectors mint and maxt contain the minimum and maximum values of the original targets.

4.4 Methodology

Different transfer functions for hidden and output layers were used to find the best ANN structure for this study. Transfer function used in hidden layer of the back propagation network is tangent-sigmoid while pure linear transfer function is used in output layer.

ANN developed for prediction of rainfall is trained with different learning algorithms, learning rates, and number of neurons in its hidden layer. The aim is to create a network which gives an optimum result. The network was simulated using 3 different Back propagation learning algorithms. They are Resilient Backpropagation (*trainrp*), Fletcher-Reeves Conjugate Gradient (*traincgf*) and Scale Conjugate Gradient (*trainscg*).

The Resilient Back propagation (*trainrp)* eliminates the effect of gradient with small magnitude. As magnitudes of the derivative have no effect on the weight update, only the sign of the derivative is used to determine the direction of the weight update. *Trainrp* is generally much faster than standard steepest descent algorithms, and require only a modest increase in memory requirements which suits network with sigmoidal transfer function.

Fletcher-Reeves Conjugate Gradient (*traincgf*) generally converges in fewer iteration than *trainrp,* although there is more computation required in each iteration. The conjugate gradient algorithms are usually much faster than variable learning rate back propagation, and are sometimes faster than *trainrp. Traincgf* also require only a little more storage than simpler algorithms, thus they are often a good choice for networks with a large number of weights.

The third algorithm, Scale Conjugate Gradient (*trainscg*) was designed to avoid the time-consuming line search. This differs from other conjugate gradient algorithm which requires a line search at each iteration. The *trainscg* routine may require more iteration to converge, but the number of computations in each iteration is significantly reduced because no line search is performed. *Trainscg* require modest storage.

4.5 Results

Daily rainfall data for 122 days in a year i.e. months June to September were chosen for training and testing. Networks were trained with data of year 1989 and tested using rainfall data of the year 1990. The training has been done using three different training functions as mentioned before: traincgf, trainrp and trainscg. Fig. 3 to Fig. 5 demonstrate the result of training with year 1989 dataset and testing with year 1990 datasets. The results are convincing and the network once trained has been tested with year 1990 datasets and the error comes out to be less than 0.005 in 5 epochs for training functions trainscg and traincgf. With trainrp function, it takes 35 iterations to train.

Another rainfall dataset is for the year 1991 and 1992, training with 1991 and testing with 1992. Fig. 6 to Fig. 8 demonstrate the result of training with year 1991 dataset and testing with year 1992 datasets. Here again, the results are convincing and the network once trained has been tested with year 1992 datasets and the error comes out to be less than 0.005 in 3 epochs for training functions trainscg and traincgf. With trainrp function, it takes 13 iterations to train.

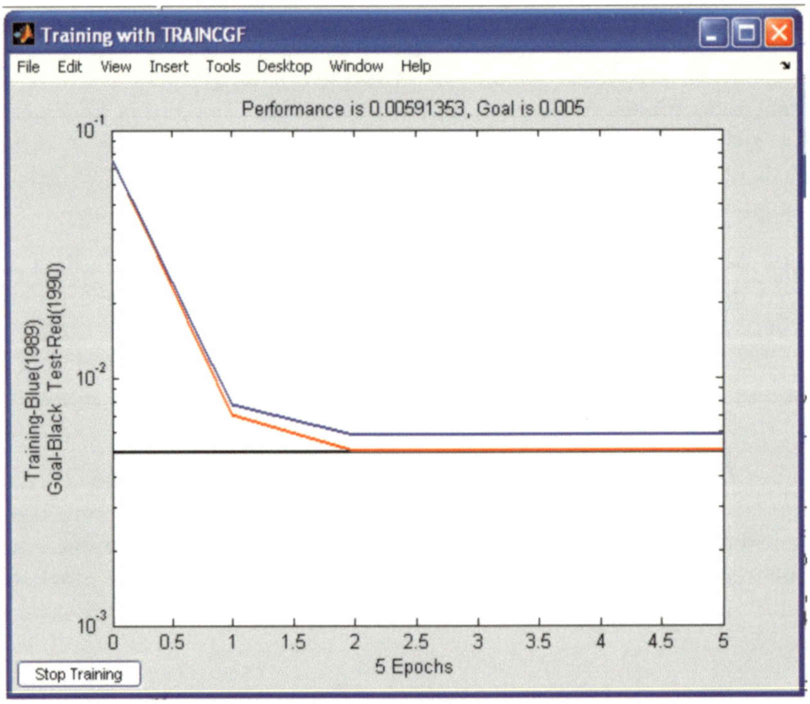

Fig. 3. Result of training ANN with Rainfall data of year 1989 and testing with Rainfall data of year 1990 using learning function traincgf

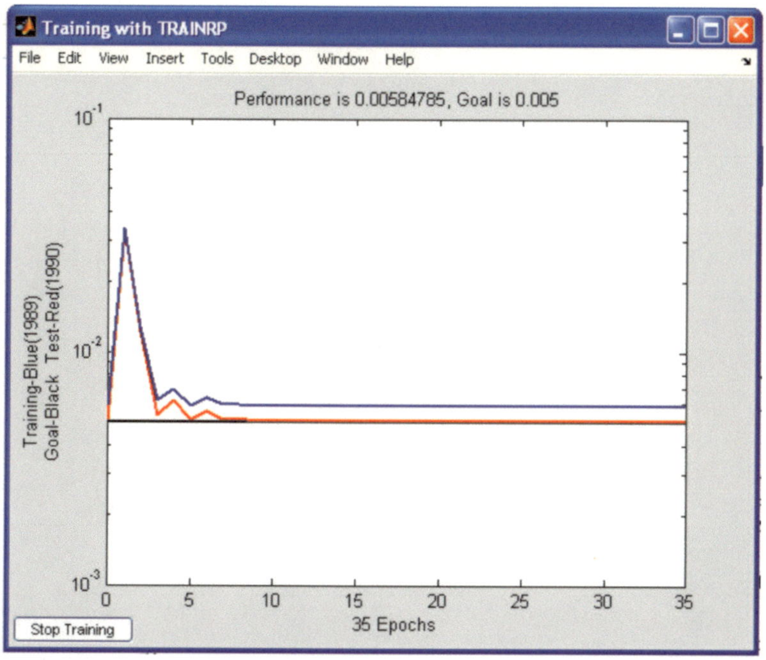

Fig. 4. Result of training ANN with Rainfall data of year 1989 and testing with Rainfall data of year 1990 using learning function trainrp

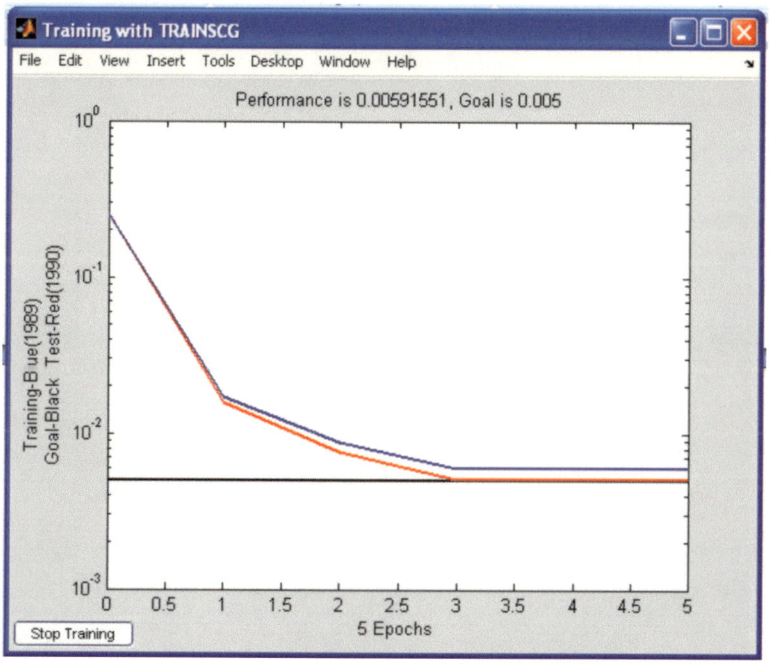

Fig. 5. Result of training ANN with Rainfall data of year 1989 and testing with Rainfall data of year 1990 using learning function trainscg

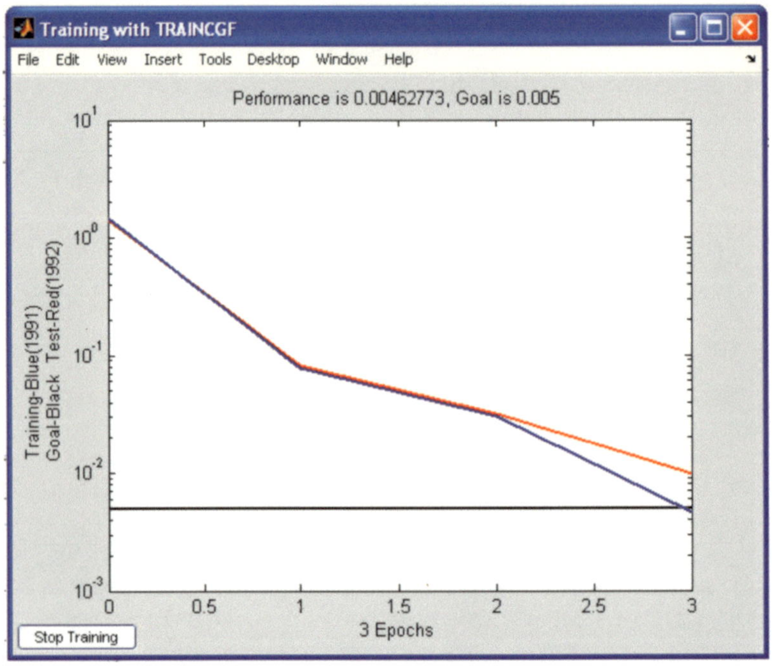

Fig. 6. Result of training ANN with Rainfall data of year 1991 and testing with Rainfall data of year 1992 using learning function traincgf

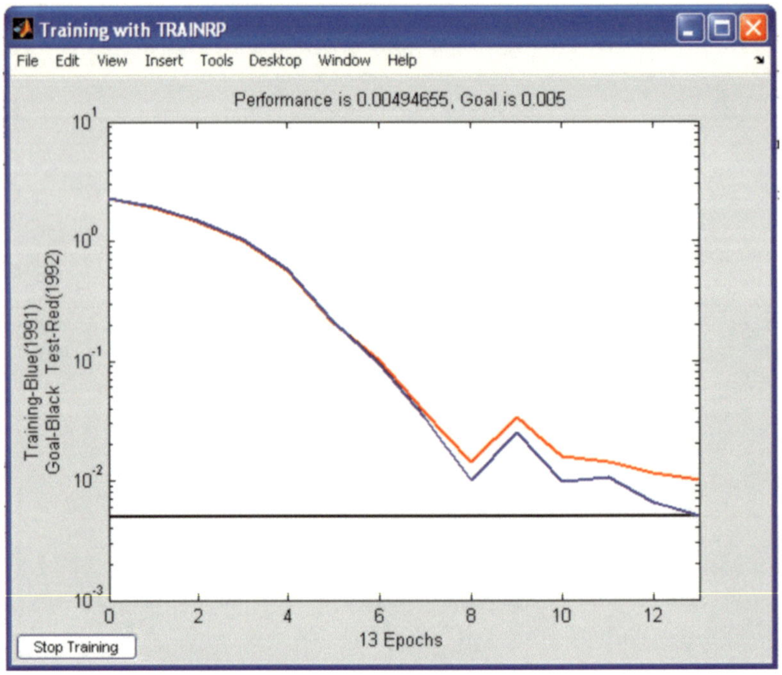

Fig. 7. Result of training ANN with Rainfall data of year 1991 and testing with Rainfall data of year 1992 using learning function trainrp

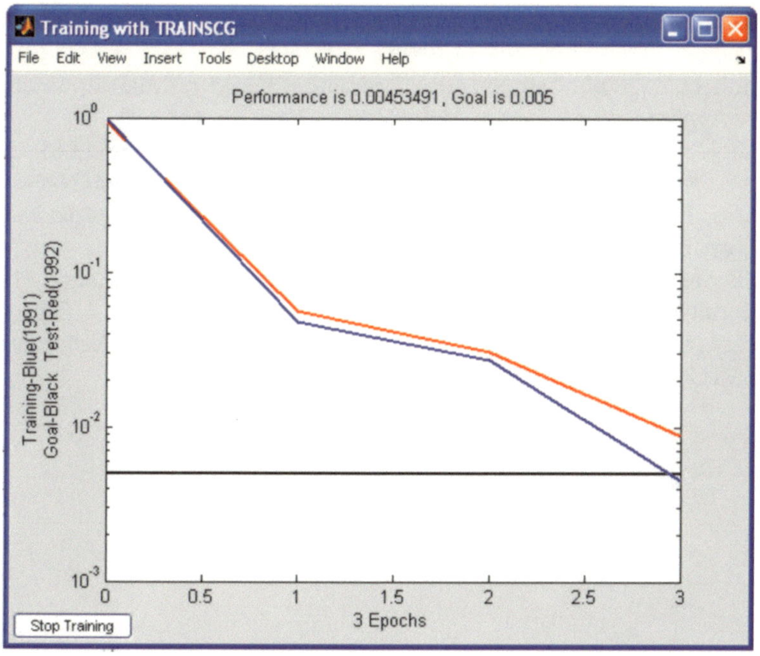

Fig. 8. Result of training ANN with Rainfall data of year 1991 and testing with Rainfall data of year 1992 using learning function trainscg

5. Conclusion

It is concluded that ANN has demonstrated promising results and is very suitable for solving the problem of rainfall forecasting. Using only the input parameters as gridded location, the ANN has been trained to predict Rainfall. This study has clearly brought out that Data Mining techniques when applied rigorously can help in providing advance information for forecast of sub-grid phenomenon.

6. Acknowledgement

This study is based on the datasets made available by courtesy of Indian Meteorological Department, India. The author is thankful for the support extended by IMD. Also, the author thanks Dr. Rattan K. Datta, Former Advisor - Deptt. of Science & Technology, Former President - Indian Meteorological Society and Computer Society of India, for his motivation and guidance.

7. References

Chattopadhyay S.(2007). Multilayered feed forward Artificial Neural Network model to predict the average summer-monsoon rainfall in India, *Journal Acta Geophysica*, Vol. 55, No.3, 2007, pp. 369-382.

Collins W., Tissot P.(2008). Use of an artificial neural network to forecast thunderstorm location, *Proceedings of the Fifth Conference on Artificial Intelligence Applications to Environmental Science,* Published in Journal of AMS., San Antonio, TX, January, 2008.

Hall T., Brooks H.E., Doswell C.A.(1999). Precipitation Forecasting Using a Neural Network, *Weather and Forecasting*, Vol. 14, 1999, pp.338-345.

Hayati M., Mohebi Z.(2007). Temperature forecasting based on neural network approach, *World Applied Sciences Journal*. Vol. 2, No. 6, 2007, pp. 613-620.

Kosko B.(2005). *Neural Networks and Fuzzy Systems*, Prentice Hall of India Ltd., 2005.

Paras, Mathur S., Kumar A., Chandra M. (2007). A Feature Based Neural Network Model for Weather Forecasting. *World Academy of Science, Engineering and Technology*, Vol. 34, 2007, pp. 66-73.

Rajeevan M., Bhate J.(2009). A high resolution daily gridded rainfall dataset (1971–2005) for mesoscale meteorological studies, *Current Science*, Vol. 96, No. 4, February 2009.

Sivanandam S.N., Sumathi S., Deepa S.N.(2009). *Introduction to Neural Networks using Matlab*, Tata McGraw Hill Education Private Ltd., 2009.

Reisinger/Roszkowski (Hrsg)

Emissionshandel